The Cry of the
CHILDREN

Kitty Havener

WESTBOW®
PRESS
A DIVISION OF THOMAS NELSON
& ZONDERVAN

Edited by
Chris Rickett
Lindsay Dankmyer
Laurie Dashnau
Betsy Swanson

Scripture quotations are from the King James Version of the Bible.

WestBow Press books may be ordered through booksellers or by contacting:

WestBow Press
A Division of Thomas Nelson & Zondervan
1663 Liberty Drive
Bloomington, IN 47403
www.westbowpress.com
1 (866) 928-1240

ISBN: 978-1-4908-9410-2 (sc)
ISBN: 978-1-4908-9411-9 (e)

Print information available on the last page.

WestBow Press rev. date: 03/07/2016

To all those who have lost their way on the road to a normal, healthy, fulfilling life: God heals all wounds. God restores hope and life comes again.

To my dear friends, Dan and Judy Buterbaugh, the loved ones whom God used to make the publishing of this book possible.

Table of Contents

Preface

There is a cry that rises from the earth and moves up into God's throne room. It falls loudly on God's ears, bringing tears to His eyes and sorrow to His heart. It causes His vengeance to come to the earth and its people.

The cry of pain God hears comes from the hearts of the children. Some of them do not understand their hearts are crying because they know nothing else. Others know something is not right, but can find no relief, so their hearts continue to cry.

God has made me hear their cry. He has made me feel their pain and know His anger. I was a child in pain and a parent who repeated these wrongs with my own children. He has made me weep before His throne for our need. *The Cry of the Children* is a result of this burden.

I write for the restoration of the children, lest God come and judge us.

> And he shall turn the heart of the fathers to the children,
> and the heart of the children to their fathers, lest I come
> and smite the earth with a curse. Mal. 4:6

Acknowledgements

To my wonderful children, who have taught me so much about parenting and life.

Chapter 1

Why Are the Children Crying?

Someone once said, "If what you are doing isn't working, change what you are doing." This sounds simple enough, but change never is. Changing the way we think or how we do things can be one of the most difficult things a human being can endeavor to do. When things are not working in life, though, change is the only answer to the problem. *The Cry of the Children* was written with the purpose of bringing about change for the good of our children–change that helps us to embrace our children with the love needed to meet their needs.

Admitting there is a problem is the first step toward change. We, as a community of adults, need to ask ourselves some serious questions about the state of our children: Are all their needs being met? Is our society, our way of living, producing children who function well in our communities? Is it possible that our ways of parenting are not producing children who grow into healthy, well-adjusted adults who are able to cope with life? We need only to watch the daily news or visit with a school principal to learn the answers to these questions. Can we say that we are producing emotionally healthy children? We have teens involved with drug and alcohol addictions, suicides, bullying, school shootings, a multitude of sexually related problems, gangs, and the list goes on. Seeing that there is a problem is a step in the direction of change.

When we honestly look at the state of today's children, we will see that we need to do something different from what we are presently doing. Change in our children's lives will take place only when we make their well-being a priority and understand what they need in order to flourish. This will come when we understand children's hearts, know how our children feel, and see the world through their eyes.

We who interact with children need to understand why the youth of today do the things they do. We need to find a solution to the problems children are facing. I have read books about people who have gone to great lengths to study and help resolve problems with animals. Monty Roberts, Mark Rashid, and Buck Brannaman are all famous for handling horses differently from everyone else and solving horses' problems by meeting a need the horses had. I have also read about the well-known man Cesar Millan, a celebrity dog trainer known as the "Dog Whisperer," who has done the same with canines. Once these men understood where the animals were coming from and what their needs were, they were able to change the horses' or the dogs' behavior. People flock to these experts to hear them teach and buy their books and videos in order to gain their knowledge. In the thirty-three years I have been a parent, I have not heard of anyone with these kinds of solutions to the problems we face with our children. Where is the person who is well-known for teaching us to understand our children to the point of revolutionary results for our children's good? We need someone to study the children, to see life from their perspectives, and learn why they behave the way they do. We need someone with the gift of caring for a person enough to understand what he or she needs and wants, and who will then supply that need. One great point to take from these experts with the animals is this: What some people viewed as a bad or evil animal was really just an animal with a need that had not been met. When the need was understood and met, the bad behavior disappeared. From these examples, we should realize that one of the worst things we can do to children is to view them as evil because of their behavior. Children's needs aren't being met, they are suffering as a result, and it shows in the way they are living out their lives.

The state of the children in our society today tells us there is something we are missing that our children need. We can clearly see this by observing their behaviors. I remember a science project that my home schooling friend did with her daughter. They made brownies several different ways, each time omitting a different ingredient. Some of the brownies weren't too bad, but most were inedible. The experiment proved that all the ingredients were essential to get the right taste and look of brownies, and when a major ingredient like flour was left out, it greatly altered how brownies turn out. This experiment is a good analogy for what we have done to our children. Parents provide many things for their children, but we have left out something major. For any child to be able to function normally in life, everything he or she needs must be provided.

I am a person who follows a recipe exactly. I like what I am making to turn out just the way it is supposed to. It is amazing that many of us haven't even begun to understand what is needed in a human life to make it complete. We see the incomplete results lived out before us every day, but do not try to fix the problem or to find out what is missing. Our children need to be given everything required in order to live life successfully. They are the ones who will follow after us and rule our world. If the next generation of people are incomplete human beings, what kind of world will there be? What kind of world do we have today? Is it a world of complete, whole, functional people? The "recipe" for a complete child is not being followed.

The cries of the children's hearts are heard in their misbehavior, negative personality traits, bad decisions, and other dysfunctional actions. Those cries tell us something is wrong. Most of us have mastered meeting our children's physical needs. We clothe them, feed them, entertain them, and buy them an abundance of things to occupy their attention. We have definitely attended to their mind's need by providing good educations for them, sometimes helping to finance their schooling through and even beyond their college years. Still, many of our children are restless, angry, bored, and frustrated. We have failed to meet a need in them that makes them complete. What is this need we've missed? For what are their hearts crying? I have written about what I believe those needs are in Chapter 2. I am a Christian, and therefore, I am writing from that perspective, but I hope every parent or caregiver of a child will hear what I have to say. First, we must begin to listen, stopping and hearing our children's cries. Then we can show we care about the children by seeking to learn what their needs are.

To help us see more clearly there is a problem, we should ask ourselves some questions about the children in our society today. Why do they love being bad? Why is it that the tougher and the meaner they are, the "cooler" they think they are? Why do they bully other kids? Why are our high school and college students drinking and experimenting with drugs? Why are teens committing suicide? Why are they apathetic toward what their parents say? Why do they give their virginity away so freely? Why don't they trust adults?

Have you ever been close enough to a group of kids to hear how they talk or what they talk about when they are uninhibited by grownups? If you want to be shocked into reality, try getting close enough to hear what our children are saying in their peer groups. Many kids today live out two personalities: one in front of adults, and another in front of their peers. When we stop and look at all of this, we can't help but ask, "How did all of this become a part of normal life?"

Being a good parent involves a whole lot more than most of us were shown by our parents and are now giving to our children. We won't raise better children by simply changing our rules or outward actions. How many of us have been down that road only to end up with another problem popping up in a different area? Finding the answers involves changing ourselves, the way we think about our kids, and our view of the whole picture of parenting. We have to see everything from an entirely different perspective. The way we have been viewing parenting has kept us from seeing our children's real needs, the result being that our children are unable to deal with the demands life places on them.

Chapter 2

What's Missing?

When we are the person producing an object or a work, we go to great lengths to gather what is needed and then proceed to create it. Car manufacturers order or build car parts; a seamstress collects a pattern, thread and material; builders buy lumber and cement; and so forth. If we leave out something, our car won't run, our clothes won't be suitable to wear, and our building will be unsafe to inhabit. This is the same common sense we need to use in raising children. We must provide all they need and be ready to give it to them, in order to create complete, well-adjusted, functional persons.

We must find out what our children are missing that is keeping them from becoming individuals who can live successful lives. We all know that our children have bodies that need food and exercise and minds that need to be educated. Why, then, don't we seem to understand that our children have another part of them that must be cared for? I am referring to the spirit that every human being possesses inside of them. Every child has a spirit, and this spirit needs care. This is the most important part of their being, but seems to be the part that is given the least attention. We have neglected a major part of the job in caring and providing for our children. This spirit part, if not cared for properly, will bring failure to every other part of our children's lives. When the spirit is cared for, it will bring healing and strength to the other areas of their life. What is the human being worth without the spirit? It is this quality that sets us apart from the rest of creation. Adding the care of the children's spirits to the other care we give them will make them complete.

Our lives do not consist of just our existence in these physical bodies living on earth. We human beings have two kinds of life inside of us. We have biological life, like the other living creatures on the earth. But we, humans made in the image of God, also have the unique quality of a spiritual life. For the purpose of this book, when referring to the spirit, I am referring to the part of a person that is eternal, the part that is left when we strip away everything that is flesh. When the body dies, what continues to live is one's spirit. It involves the heart, personality, thoughts, and what some call the soul. In *The Cry of the Children,* I do not wish to just talk about regenerated (saved) spirits or souls. I desire to make everyone see the importance of understanding that we all have a spirit and it needs care just like the other parts of our life do. I take the view that the only answer to finding real life for our spirit is in knowing God through Jesus Christ.

> This is eternal life, that they might know thee, the only true God; and Jesus Christ, whom thou hast sent.
> John 17:3

I also hope and pray that when people become more spirit-minded they will see their need of God. Regardless of whether one is saved or unsaved, though, each person still has a spirit. Why should we live our lives with no regard for the spirit part of us? Do we not hear that spirit crying out within ourselves because of our neglect of it?

When looking at all the children's needs–mental, physical, and spiritual– what do we see are the basic ingredients children need to live life successfully? From the moment of birth, there are two places in our children screaming to be fed: their stomachs and their spirits. We know what their stomachs want. In *The Cry of the Children,* we will look for what the spirit is crying out.

By properly caring for your children's spirits, parents enable their children to be whole. Caring for our children's spirits must be seen as a priority. If children do not receive this, they will be wounded and sick in their spirits, which will cause them to function improperly in life. Parents must give attention to their children's spirits as much as, if not more than, they care for their children's minds and bodies. That spirit is the source from which they live the rest of their lives. Parents must know what the spirit requires in order to be healthy and to thrive just as much as they must know what children's bodies need in order to be healthy and to function properly. What parent does not realize that too much junk food is unhealthy for their children? Most of us know fruits and vegetables will make our children's body strong. But do parents know what their children's spirits need in order to thrive? What caregiver of children does not understand that children should not play in the street? The caregiver understands the danger. These same parents and caregivers must also recognize the potential threats to their children's spirits. What might bring harm to a child's spirit? The spirit needs attention; it needs to be watched over, guided, instructed, and fed properly, just like their bodies and minds. I have found that understanding the needs in my own spirit helped me in seeing the needs my children had in their spirits. I see a great need in my spirit for peace. I know I need that calm in me so I can face the demands of life. Our children need peace in their spirits too, especially as they are developing their personalities. Learning they can have inner peace is important. Also, when going back and remembering how I felt in different situations in my childhood, I realize what I wanted and needed at the time helped me better understand the needs of my children. I remember desperately wanting my mom to show me she loved and accepted me. I just wanted her to do something that said to me, "You're mine and you're okay." These are two examples of how we can identify what spiritual needs our children are facing in their lives.

We need to consider our children's spiritual needs daily, hourly, even moment by moment. What are the needs of our children's spirits right now? Have they been attended to today? Are their spirits healthy, or are they plagued with problems? We can prepare our children spiritually to face each day. We can teach, nurture, and protect their spirits every day. Let us come to the knowledge that our children's eternal spirits should be our top priority. It is the part of them that will stand before God when their lives are over and all else has passed away. We spend so much time, energy, and money on our children's physical lives, so much effort building their bodies and their brains, but neither will pass into eternity with them. Only their spirits will live eternally, in whatever states they are. We need to attend to this part of our children at all times. We need to give our own spirits attention daily. If we are Christians, this is the place where the Holy Spirit comes to dwell in us. Is it an honored place or an ignored place? In this day and age, in what condition are our spirits? And if we are not caring well for our own spirits, chances are we are not caring for or giving value to our children's spirits. Most know what is required of parents for the physical and mental care of their children. Do we know what is expected of parents when it comes to caring for their children's eternal spirits? We need to begin to see that our children's problems in life may have their source in their pitifully neglected spirits.

Children whose spirits are not nurtured and cared for or are just ignored will not develop as whole people. These children will not be able to face the demands made on their lives. As previously stated, when the spirit is healthy, the body, mind, and personality thrive. Because we all too often have neglected our own and our children's spirits, the rest of our lives have been corrupted. When our physical bodies are sick, can we function correctly? When we are mentally ill, it influences all the rest of our life. What are the horrid effects on our lives or our children's lives because of the serious neglect of our and their spirits? Understanding where our problems are coming from is vital to finding a solution.

> Keep thy heart with all diligence; for out of it are the
> issues of life. Prov. 4:23

According to *Vine's Expository Dictionary of New Testament Words* (pages 546-547, unabridged edition, by W. E. Vine, M.A. MacDonald Publishing Company, McLean, Virginia 22010), "the heart is the seat of moral and spiritual life." We live our lives out from our hearts (where our spirits reside), so if our hearts are in healthy condition, our lives will reflect that.

I want to look again at where our attention as parents is focused today. We put major emphasis on education. College is seen as a necessity, but what about the condition of our bodies? We often give them valuable time and attention, too. We have sports programs, dance, martial arts, and the YMCA, all for our children to participate in so that they can become strong physically. But what about our children's hearts, where their spirits reside? What attention is given to them? The church, if the gospel is presented in a way that meets the true needs of the heart, can help parents provide for needs of their children's spirits, but it is not a substitute for parents attending to their children's spiritual needs.

The sad, incomprehensible fact is that we expect our children to function acceptably in life after we have failed to care for their spirits. Too often we don't understand why little Johnny or Susie won't meet our expectations of good behavior. We have tried everything: discipline, grounding, removal of electronics, lectures (don't ask my children about those), and our own and others' prayers. Yet it is bizarre to think that we expect children to act and to perform acceptably when they have not been given even the basic needs for their spirits. We are demanding something from them they do not have the capacity to give us: the behaviors and temperaments of well-adjusted human beings. So what do we do because they can't behave "normally"? We discipline them, scold them, and take them to counselors. I have known many parents who, upon the recommendation of their doctors or school officials, put their children on medication to help control their behavior. While doing so may occasionally be warranted, I am not sure our children are getting the right message when we are quick to give them prescriptions in elementary school in attempt to solve their problems and then turn around and tell them to "Just say no" to drugs in middle school. Might this actually be contributing to the drug problem we have with the teens today? Wouldn't it be easier for us to meet all the needs of our children than keep trying to deal with problems stemming from their needs not being met?

Any living creature that has not had all of its needs met will suffer in some way. One cannot successfully teach a suffering creature anything. Can one walk up to a sick, wounded dog and say, "Now boy, I am going to teach you to fetch"? Such a one would probably get bitten. Is it not also true that one cannot expect one's child to be able to learn properly when it has a need or a wound in some part of his or her life? I wonder how many of us have been "bitten" by our children when we have tried to teach them correct behavior or discipline them. Many of us have been "bitten" by our teenagers when we tried to address their unacceptable behavior. Unfortunately, we are often trying to deal with an outward manifestation of a neglected hurting spirit, all the while demanding that our children act like perfectly well-adjusted human beings. Parenting this way will greatly frustrate our children. If continued, it will destroy the relationship between us and our children. Our children cannot change until someone identifies and deals with their problem or problems. When our children's spirits are not cared for from birth, they will be screaming for help. We will then spend our lives and energy as parents dealing with problem after problem (in the physical realm) stemming from our children's neglected spirits. If our children have parts of their lives that are needy and sick, we have to take care of these needs before our children can learn and mature.

Children start their lives physically and mentally handicapped, so to speak. They can neither get up and walk around and take care of themselves, nor can they communicate their needs. Babies can cry because they are hungry, but they cannot tell us what they need in words. As a child gets older, he learns how to identify his physical needs and put them into words so that other people understand and can meet them. My sixteen-month-old grandson says, "Na, na, na" and we know he wants a banana. The ability to identify the need in our heart or spirit and put that into words is, however, an ability that few of us have learned. If we are a generation that pays very little attention to our children's spirits, what will we know about what is going on in their spirits? Yet many adults expect children to have this ability. When dealing with a problem child, I have heard parents and teachers ask, "Why didn't this child tell me what was bothering him or her?" When doing so, they are asking children to perform a task that some adults haven't mastered. Even if children could look within themselves and evaluate why they feel the way they do, some do not know how to name the negative emotions they are feeling and then act out abnormally because they aren't aware of any alternatives. But their actions speak loudly enough for everyone to hear, saying, "I have a problem." As children grow up, they would have to be trained extensively in psychology to be able to express in words what is going on in their hearts and minds. No children are trained this way. Even as teenagers, kids cannot always articulate what is going on inside of them. This is understandable, as many of us adults have a hard time understanding ourselves at times. I remember a lady I worked with telling me, as she was leaving work to go home, "I can go home and get away from everyone else who bugs me, but I can't get away from myself." She seemed very frustrated with her inability to make herself someone she wanted to be around. God has an answer for this problem. That is why He gave us his Holy Spirit to come live in our spirits. I have gained more wisdom and understanding about what was going on in my spirit from God than I have from anything else I tried. I know listening to the wisdom the Holy Spirit gives works because as I dealt with the problem areas the Holy Spirit showed me in my spirit, my life changed and the problems I was facing went away. One of the big pillars of my faith is seeing the unbelievable changes God has made in my heart. God makes our hearts a place of comfort to us instead a place that causes us pain.

The problems in our spirits and our children's spirits can be dealt with and resolved when we give care and attention to them and seek God for the answers.

What happens when we neglect children's spirits from birth? It is the same thing that will happen when we neglect anything; it grows weak, sick, and decays. The minds and bodies receiving care grow and mature, but the spirits inside wither. Perhaps the problem is that no one tended our spirits, and as a consequence, we don't know how to tend to our children's spirits. Much of what is happening with the children of our nation today (drugs, violence, crime, younger and younger criminals) is a result of our children's spirits screaming, "I'm sick!" We parents are so busy with our own lives that we cannot hear these cries. Maybe adults today are too preoccupied trying to meet the needs of their own wounded, starving, and uncared for spirits. Sadly, the next generation growing up is even less cared for then our present one. If this neglect continues, each generation will be sicker than the one it follows. Where will we all end up if we don't fix this problem?

There is no more dangerous thing, as far as I am concerned, than a child who has a wounded spirit. This neglected, uncared for child will grow into an individual that can destroy the world we love and live in. The news is full of examples of such unhealthy persons. The pain is so great to them that they are screaming through their destructive actions, "Somebody feel my pain; somebody care about my needs; somebody help me!" If we adults listen, we can hear the needy children say through their actions, "I hurt inside. I can't stand the pain, nobody cares, and no one will listen. They need to feel my pain, so I will make them suffer like I do!" This is the cry of a child who was given life but never given care for his or her spirit. The top items on the list for care of the spirit are making sure children know they are valued and loved by us. These spiritually neglected children are sending a message loud and clear. Someone destroyed their spirits by not giving them love and value, so they feel compelled to return that destruction to others. Then we hear their scream. This is the cry at the root of the heart of many a violent criminal. The individual was telling us this truth about their misery, over and over in many ways to many people before he or she committed a heinous crime, but nobody listened. No one that miserable is silent in their actions, and there is a price to pay for not listening to a crying child. It will revert to other means of being heard. Ignoring the cry of a wounded soul only creates a bigger problem that wreaks havoc on the family and all the rest of society.

We seem to think that we have done all that is necessary to have the good life. We may ask ourselves, "What is going on, anyway? What happened to the ideal life of getting married, having children, and living happily ever after?" Again I state, we have put all our attention on the state of our flesh and forgotten that we have spirits that require care. Each generation that ignores this becomes more ill as the result of neglect. Nevertheless, we try to live normal lives the way we are, wondering what happened when a kid goes to our local school and shoots his classmates and teachers. Should not a tragedy such as this wake us up?

A dead person is nothing but a flesh vessel (frame) without a spirit. The body decays. But the spirit lives forever. Why, oh why, do we spend more time caring for the temporary part? Why do we not nurture and care for our children's spirits? If I have learned anything by watching the children of this world, it is there is an enemy out there whose main purpose is to attack and kill the spirit. I watch him work overtime, day after day, to beat away at a child's hope and self-confidence until they give up. This enemy is relentless. He knows what the most valuable part of us is, and he aims his weapons right at it. Where are the walls that protect our children from such an enemy? Where is the army who should stand guard over their souls? We have no such army, and as a result the enemy has come in and is destroying our precious little ones' souls. My one and only purpose in writing *The Cry of the Children* is to see children once again nurtured and protected from the destroyer of their souls. It is our job as parents, teachers, and adults.

Nevertheless, if you are beginning to see the results of your neglect in this area, I would like to throw a rope of hope out to you. I have felt the despair of this situation and know its pain. God has been in the business of healing and restoring spirits of all ages for a long time. But oh, if we just did the job required of us, how much pain we could save our children.

Review:

- Our children are not okay
- Our children's actions are the only cry we will hear, as children do not have the words to express the pain that they feeling
- Our children's problem behavior comes from their neglected spirits, not from their well-fed bodies or their educated minds

- Children with unkempt spirits cannot learn or function properly in other areas of life
- The greatest problem is that we do not understand how to meet the needs of the children's spirits
- There is hope, for God will help us learn to meet the needs for our children

Chapter 3

The Key Ingredient

Where do you keep your family jewels or valuable papers? Many people go to the bank and rent a safety deposit box for their valuable items. There these items are put in a locked box and then placed in a huge safe in the bank. The bank has guards and alarm systems to aid in protecting people's valuable items. We know the worth of our treasures and want to take good care of them. They are safe because we invest all that is necessary to guarantee it. When we place great value on something, our actions automatically come right behind with what is needed to assure that this item of admiration is taken care of.

What value do we place on the tiny, precious, human lives, laid in our arms on the days of their births? Every human spirit must be given a proper position of worth on which to stand. God gives it to us by creating us and giving us life. He establishes that we are creatures of value, ones dearly loved by Him. Parents, this is on what we are to build. I am separating the basic self-worth that God gives to every human life from us knowing we all have a sinful nature that separates us from God and must be dealt with through faith in Jesus Christ when we are old enough to understand the Gospel. However, we have worth to God whether we are saved or unsaved. The value God places on every human life is steadfast and unchanging, evident in the great price paid to restore us to Him. It is we who do not value our lives and others lives as God does.

Do we take the actions necessary to prove that our children's self-worth is a valuable asset? From the very start of their lives, our actions should show how much that we treasure and hold dear our precious children. The best way to do this is by building a healthy self-image within their spirits–one that will support them through the many changes and challenges of life. Our children will learn (though I would rather use the word "catch" here because it is a more unconscious act than learning) from us how much we value their lives and then treat themselves accordingly. We spend day after day telling and showing them how much worth they have to us and this creates in them the value they have for themselves. From their infancy to the days they graduate school, in every tiny little detail of their lives, we communicate from our spirit to theirs the extent to which we value them. How can we help our children have a strong sense of self-worth from the very start of their lives? A proper self-worth is needed in a child's spirit even before he or she is born. A pregnant mother's spirit can communicate this through the mother's thoughts and attitudes. She must first, however, establish the value of her child in her own heart and mind.

I want to present the case on behalf of an unborn child. I am specifically going to present this to you as if the child is talking to its Mommy.

Hi, Mommy.
Who am I? To whom do I belong? What is my value? Will you give me the answers? I need so badly to know. You see, the answers to those questions will set the course of my life. Even now, Mommy, we communicate–your spirit with mine. I long to hear you say, "This is my child; I love this life." Please don't view me as an accident or say, "I didn't need this." For even now, my sense of self-worth begins.

My life has just begun, and you, Mommy, are the one who announces to the world who I am: a blessing or a curse, accepted or rejected, valued or neglected. Maybe you don't see or understand that you, Mommy, set the stage for my well-being while I grow here in inside you. The spirit of love or rejection enters my being even now.

I am developing here in this safe place. You and Daddy prepare my room and make plans for my life. I have a bed, a stroller, toys, and lots of clothes. There is something else, though, that I need from you more than anything else. Will you show me what my value in this world is? Please tell my little spirit it is cherished and loved. Please satisfy my need to be completely accepted. That's for what I really want and long.

Please see me as a good thing that you can enjoy and not as a demand on your time and energy. Whatever you choose to believe about me, I also will believe about me. My spirit will be a blank slate, and all you communicate to me will be how I come to know who I am. What will you tell me? Will I know I am okay and secure, that I belong to you, or will I never be sure and instead be made to live life in that frailty of spirit? When others in my life come against me, will I be able to fall back on the value you gave me, or will I fail because I don't know who I am?

Oh, Mommy, you can forget the toys and all the accessories, all your plans of providing what I might need. Right now please let me know that you love me and that I am important to you. That's what will make me strong. I can face anything knowing you love and value me.

Your little child

How I wish I had understood the true needs of a child's spirit before I had my children. These needs had not been met in me as a child, though, and I therefore had no idea what my children needed. I went to great extremes making sure my children had everything else. I beat myself up emotionally when I messed up and my children had to go without something I thought they needed. I didn't understand that I was missing the one thing they needed the most. Their spirits needed to know love, value, and acceptance.

Mothers, we must understand that meeting the need of our children's spirits is one of our first responsibilities as parents. We must place great importance on this requirement. Forget the nursery preparations, the baby shower, and the sonogram for the moment. First and foremost, a child's little spirit is crying out from the womb, "What is the value of my life?" Pregnancy is a very crucial time during which to start communicating value to our children. To not understand the importance of it would be to inflict the first wound on the spirit of the tiny person that is looking to us for life. I know mothers who said throughout their pregnancies, "I don't want this child" or "It is a real inconvenience in my life right now." "It" is a life, a child, not a sickness or problem.

Moreover, a child is not born with a full stomach or a satisfied spirit. It is born with hunger, physical and spiritual. The body screams for food and the spirit searches for its worth and purpose. We have no problem fulfilling the stomach's need to stop the crying, but do we even notice that searching little spirit looking for worth?

After our child is born, we have to go through each stage of life with the child, communicating the same thing: "You have worth, you are a valuable person; I treasure your existence." It is more difficult to do this at some ages than at others. The toddler years, a time when children explore everything and run everywhere, is a time when one must take special care to convey this positive message. It takes extra effort to make sure that toddlers understand that they are loved and accepted amidst the constant "No's." Granted, saying "No" at this age is important in order to teach toddlers boundaries so that they do not maim themselves or break everything in the house. To counteract all these negatives, though, we must use great positive reinforcement. We should constantly be aware of the message our children are receiving about themselves from us. The teenage years are another challenging time to communicate self-worth to children. I will say, though, that if you have been practicing proper positive parenting for years, your teen will be ready for the assault on their self-esteem that often occurs at this age. However, if we have not prepared our teens with the message, "You are valuable people" prepare for a very rough ride. Just get on your knees now and beg God to give you grace (daily, hourly). We can really make a disaster of our kids' lives by not giving them what they need to survive. That can come back and hit us in the face during their teenage years. It is the harvest time of parenting, if you will. All the years of what we have said, done, and taught come to full bloom when the teenage years commence. But our blind spot is inherent in the fact that we do not blame what we contributed when it all goes wrong; instead, we blame our kids for not behaving acceptably. Getting across the message of value and self-worth to our children in the different stages of their childhood requires concentrated effort.

When children do not develop a proper healthy self-worth, they face the world with a deep wound. It is a wound that the enemy of our souls uses to bring great harm to their lives. It is the path that so easily leads to destruction. View not giving your children's spirits value and worth as if you had never fed your children a proper diet during their childhood, while their physical bodies was forming and growing. Their bodies would have developed without the proper vitamins and minerals needed for organs to form and to function properly and would not be able to fight off disease and sickness. Their physical bodies will be sick and this will affect how they live every other part of their lives. It will affect them emotionally, mentally, psychologically, and socially. If we understand that a person who has been taught they have no value to others will result in person with a deficiency in their spirit, then we will hopefully not neglect this need in our children. When their spirits lack what they need to be whole and healthy, the rest of their lives are dysfunctional, their view of life is skewed, and then their decisions are destructive. These wounded people then live in unhealthy states of being, and every area of their existence is affected negatively.

The difference between children whose self-worth has been established and the ones who has been left hanging in what I call "identity oblivion" is quite evident. I have seen it firsthand: children who had no consideration given to their self-worth, but rather had their negative behaviors pointed out over and over again. I've seen these children become adults and this lack of worth then acted as the eyeglasses through which they viewed their world. The lack of self-worth is a wound in their spirits that when an experience in life touched

19

it, it caused a very negative, destructive reaction. On the other hand, I have seen children whose parents made deliberate efforts, from day one, to let their little ones know they were loved and accepted by them. These children's good behavior was praised and the bad behaviors were always handled with kind instruction and assistance. These children faced their lives with a sense of confidence that was alluring to others. These children were like magnets to others who wanted to draw from these children's strength and stability. When negative situations came up in these children's lives, these children's inner strength never wavered. These children were able to see the challenging and difficult times for what they were and deal with them properly.

Parents, God has given us a huge responsibility. Our children gain self-worth when they know we value their lives, when we genuinely love them, and when we accept them unconditionally. Consequently, these are the pillars that support our children's self-worth. These strengths need to start being established while our children are still in the womb. The more time that goes by without this message being communicated, the harder it will be to establish a sense of self-worth in our children's lives. The natural negative forces of life will start to work against our children's spirits and destroy their proper sense of self-worth. Thus, our efforts in this area are crucial to our children's well-being.

Chapter 4

Listening to Your Child

We all have ears for the purpose of hearing sounds. Greater yet is the gift of being able to hear with our hearts. The truth of the latter statement impressed on me anew one night when I was sitting on the couch exhausted from all my daily duties of motherhood and ministry. I was finishing folding some laundry while I zoned out by watching television. My children had been put to bed and I felt the relief all parents feel at the end of a busy day when one's little ones are settled down for the night and one has a few minutes to call one's own. Then, from the bedroom came a call: "Mom, will you come here?" At first, I whined in self-pity at the prospect of facing another demand being placed on me after an already long day. The call came again. This time I caught something in the call that spoke to my heart and spirit that said, "Answer the call." I got up and went back to the bedroom to see what my child needed. When I went to her bedside, my daughter said to me, "Mom, I want to pray and believe in Jesus." In all the years that have passed since this happened, I have never stopped being thankful that I listened to my child's cry that night with my heart instead of with my weary mind.

Listening to children with our hearts not only means being available at all times, but also means listening carefully to all that is being spoken–and to what is not being spoken. Do we truly understand exactly what our children are saying to us when they talk to us? Can we go beyond understanding what they are saying with their mouths and decode what they are saying in their spirits? When we listen to their words with our ears, we are interpreting what is being said through our brains. When we listen to what their spirits are saying, we will get the real message. Parents, we have to acquire the ability to hear what our children are really saying. To do this, we first need to get rid of our preconceived notions of what we think our children need to know so that when they talk to us, we do not give them canned answers. Then, we need to keep silent (often the most difficult part) and watch them over a period of time and in different life situations. This requires a major investment of our time, yet it is what we do when we truly love something. We watch, we learn, we think about what we learned. This takes even more time. We need to ask ourselves, "What are my children really saying?" and "Are they communicating that something is not right with them?" We need to get close enough to them to hear what their spirits are saying. All this time and energy we are spending on our children will also communicate to them (without words) the fact that they are valuable to us. That is an extra bonus.

We misinterpret much of what people, especially our children, are trying to tell us about themselves. We need to be quiet, wait, and watch. This is what the dog and horse whisperer do with the animals: observe. They study the animals' habits, histories, and needs as well as what caused them to react in one way or another. The whisperers are smart enough not to do anything to "correct" a problem until they had fully studied the subject and the situation. We need to do this with our children. Many of us jump right in by speaking harshly to and punishing our children and end up making matters worse. When parenting, we need to be like God. He forgives us repeatedly, is the author of patience, and gives us a long time to learn what He is teaching us. He knows we are slow learners and that we tend to forget much of what He has told us over and over again. If only we could give our children the same grace

22

that God gives us. With this grace, we will never forget to instruct our children patiently, positively, and kindly. We must take the time to discover what the real problems are and understand what our children are trying to communicate before we react.

We need to meditate on what we observe in our children, take notes, ask God for wisdom (James 1:5), and read books about parenting. We should not jump in blindly and try to handle problems that our children are having. We should study the situations as if they were the most important problems of our lives. When we have given them the time and quality attention they deserve, then tackle them. Remember that they are lives, not objects, not reflections of us, and not possessions. They are living beings with eternal spirits. What in this world could be more valuable: our cars, our houses, our golf games, our friends? I could go on, but we know that there is nothing of more value than the life of a living human being, especially the ones we brought into the world and care for. My daughter has taught me much about parenting by telling me what she has learned about working with horses. One of those things is that you never communicate to the horse you are working with that you are in a hurry. Instead, you should always act like you have all the time in the world. What is the point? In acting this way, you are communicating to the creature, "You are so valuable. Take and use all the time you need from me." To apply this analogy well, we should take the time needed to handle our children with great care.

Additionally, we need to be careful not to jump to conclusions with or about our children. One of the most discouraging things in my life is when people who do not know me well judge me wrongly for my actions. Oftentimes what we do or say can be completely misunderstood by people who do not know us or from where we are coming. God says,

Judge not. Matt. 7:1

He knows that we cannot see another person's heart, and therefore, that we have no business making a judgment. There have been times in my life when I have done something, with no evil intent, and someone has completely misinterpreted it as being nasty. I could see how it

23

appeared that way to him or her, but that individual could not see that he or she was misunderstanding the situation. This principle applies to our children. We should not judge them wrongly–not their motives or their actions. This maxim requires much time and observation of who our children are. We have to be careful because if we do judge them wrongly, we may be communicating to them that we think they are evil or have evil intentions. We do not want our children to think we view them as evil. We should not even go down this road. It will lead us to destruction and devastation. I am not saying that a child cannot do evil; we live in a fallen world, our children's behavior sometimes being part of that. (However) I am saying that we do not want to communicate to our children that we view them as evil people. Would we want that thought woven into the fabric of our children's personalities? We do not want to be the parents of children who view themselves as evil. It helps, when dealing with problems in behavior, to make sure we understand that the problems have a source and finding the causes of the behaviors is where we should put our focus, not on blaming our children.

The precious gifts of freedom and truth are crucial when dealing with our children. We need to always remember to give our children the freedom to be themselves, but never fail to let them experience the fruit of their choices. We should get rid of the images in our heads of what you think our children should be. I am referring to individual personalities, not normal standards of childhood behavior. People thrive on freedom. We can give our children a free place to live, grow, and experience life. When we enslave them to what we want them to be, there is the danger that they will never find out who they were created to be. Does God make carbon copies? Consider snowflakes, fingerprints, and many other unique examples of creation. God is the one who created our children, not us. Let's teach our children to live truthfully, live our lives truthfully in front of them, and then have the courage to set them free to walk their lives out their way. The path to God is the way of truth. We cannot teach our children to live a lie or to pretend to be different from what they really are in order to please us. They very well could just pretend their whole lives and never learn to be their true selves. If so, what will they do when they face God, having faked it their whole lives? Life is best lived truthfully, facing who we really are and dealing with it. We need to let our children be themselves. If there are problems, we need to find the source and fix them. If all is well, we should thank God. In any case, freedom and truth will enable our children to have healthy spirits.

Chapter 5

Building Our Children an Ark

Noah heard God speak to him, believed what he heard, and went to do something about what God had told him. He built a giant boat and filled it with his family and animals of every kind. It took a very long time and was not easy to do, but as a result of Noah's action, humanity and all other living creatures survived the flood that covered the entire earth. We can all thank God and Noah for keeping human and animal life safe from extinction during the world's worst storm.

It is no secret that the ferocious storms of life will hit our children during their lifetimes. We can help our children to build an ark, a place of safety, to order to keep them when the floods of trouble come. They must have a safe place to run to when the things of this world, built on life in the flesh, fail them. If our children do not have a haven to run to, they will sink and perish. Both you and I have watched negative circumstances come and destroy people's lives. I have seen people who never recover from their problems and start a downward spiral of bad decisions that they can't find their way out of. Families fall apart, people give up, and life becomes hopeless. Knowing the truth, that problems will come is not the problem. Not preparing our children for these bad situations in life is often the real problem. No amount of food and exercise will enable them to face the emotional disturbances that come with life. No amount of education will get them through some of the losses we suffer in this life. What can we build in our children which will enable them to face the troubles of life? We can build strong spirits within them. These strong spirits can serve as our children's place of safety that keeps them alive and strong through whatever their lives bring.

We are to use the time we have with our children to prepare them to go out and live in the world by themselves, and then to survive and thrive there. Most of us in the United States are able to provide what children need to keep their bodies strong and their minds able to function in a vocation. We can also provide for our children spiritually by giving them a place to draw hope from when the world beats them down. Then, when their bodies get sick or their jobs end, they will have the support of their spirits to keep them. We adults all know that life is often hard to handle. Our kids need a safe, secure place to keep their soul when things in life go the wrong direction. We have only a few brief years to get our children ready to face living in this world all on their own.

Noah's ark was a place of safety for his family and all the animals of the earth. It held pairs of animals so that they could replenish the earth after the storm passed. The ark held the souls and bodies of man. It held food and seeds with which to replant the earth. Is the ark not a picture of what we must prepare for our children's lives? We usually spend a minimum of eighteen years building and filling our children's spirits with what they are going to need: confidence, courage, hope, faith, purpose. All of these things are kept in the spirits of the children, not in their bodies or their minds. All of these things are what sustains life when trouble comes. Our children's spirits are the safe places where we can stockpile all that they will need for their lives.

How we handle the problems in our life can make us or break us. You and I have watched people whose lives hit the rocks of disaster. When they cannot handle it, they react out of despair and hopelessness and sometimes wreck their lives. Then, there they lie, broken in pieces.

We have also met people who suffer the same troubles in their lives and yet remain strong in spirit. They have a safe place that they have built for their spirits in God, and they run there and stay strong. They make it through the disaster and their lives become stronger because of it. Will our children be the tomorrow's "wrecked" adults or resilient adults? What they have stored in their spirits will be the determining factor.

We spend so much of life building the things that we think we need. Let us remember again what lives forever. It is not the body that we feed and exercise, not the mind that we educate and fill with facts and memories, but the spirit that we nurture and cherish. Therefore, we need to be all the more diligent in building our children a place of safety by providing the things they need to have strong spirits. Everything we build in the spirit will last for eternity, making this place one of great value.

> For we know that if our earthly house of this tabernacle were dissolved, we have a building of God, a house not made with hands, eternal in the heavens. 2 Cor. 5:1

Chapter 6

A Message to Fathers

Why is the *Cry of the Children* important to you, a father? Luke 1: 1-17 is a record of when Gabriel came to tell Zechariah about the birth of his son, John the Baptist. We read in verse 17,

> And he [John] shall go before him [Christ] in the spirit and power of Elijah, to turn the hearts of the fathers to the children, and the disobedient to the wisdom of the just; to make ready a people prepared for the Lord. Luke 1:17

John was to go before Christ and prepare the way–"to make ready a people prepared." What an important job! But how was a mere man to prepare the way for the Son of God to walk among the people on the earth? "In the spirit and power of Elijah" means, of course, through the Holy Spirit's power. In this power, one thing he was to do was "turn the hearts of the fathers to the children." Now, think about this: John, who Jesus said was the greatest of the Old Testament prophets (Matt. 11:11), was given the job of preparing the way for the Son of God to come to earth and minister to humankind. How could people best prepare for such a great event? John was chosen to teach the fathers to turn their heart to their children. From this, we see that God definitely cares about what value fathers place on their children.

The message to fathers found in Luke 1 can be summed up as such: Fathers, loving your children is far more important than you may have thought it was. This message is also found in Malachi, the very last words of the Old Testament. It stands to reason that the last words spoken by God in the Old Testament must be very important–and He spoke them to the fathers. It says there also: Fathers, you are to turn your hearts to the (your) children. This was part of the preparation for Christ (the New Testament) to come and minister to the world: fathers loving their children, again. God repeated it and so I'm going to: in order to prepare the way for Christ to minister to this world, fathers, you need to love your children; you need to turn your hearts to them. Your hearts should be full of: love, affection, kindness, compassion, and care. This means that children must be your first interest, not your last. It means that your hearts' affections are set on them and their needs, that they take precedence over everything else in your life (except, perhaps, your wife). It means that you know your children well and watch them closely. You must know when they are hurt and know what moves them towards goodness, as well as what leads them towards evil. You have spent valuable time with them and know their interests. You ought to have been there for them enough for them to trust you. The key is your children knowing that they are never alone and that they can always depend on you for help. They must know that you would sooner give your life to protect them than to see them hurt. You must consider them valuable and accept them as they are. You must believe that your love for them will conquer anything bad in them. The Word of God tells us plainly that fathers loving their children is invaluable to God.

What are the standards for the fathers in today's world? We have fathers occupied with many things: watching sports, hanging out with their friends, and pursuing their careers, to name a few. Turning your hearts towards your children means fathers are to be concerned about what is going on in the lives of their children. Dads need to understand how to love their children. When you love something, this love compels you to live a certain way as to meet the needs of the person or thing you love. Fathers, watch where you place your love, because you will just naturally gravitate towards spending your time and energy meeting the needs of your object of love. In Joel 3, when judgment on the nations, which will take place at the end of this world, is pronounced, one of the great sins that brought it about is recorded. This sinful act is at the opposite end of the way God wants us to view our children. Verse three reads:

> ... they have casts lots for my people; and have given a boy for a harlot, and sold a girl for wine, that they might drink. Joel 3:3

Here the great sin is man selling children so he can experience pleasure. This demonstrates how God views our children and how He expects us to treat them. We are to treat them with great respect and care. Unfortunately, many fathers seek to please their own interests at the expense of meeting the needs of their children. Fathers are to turn their hearts to their children, not to their own pleasure.

There is another important scripture that speaks to fathers. In this verse we find a warning to fathers concerning their children:

> Ye, fathers, provoke not your children to wrath: but bring them up in the nurture and admonition of the Lord. Eph. 6:3

How do fathers provoke their children to wrath? I have known no greater anger than that of unloved and neglected children. Children who are not valued are angry children. They not only hate their own lives but hate those who have been given what they were denied: value and worth. They have been cheated out of real life. They have been given a physically life but denied a spiritual life. They are forced to live a torturous half-life, never really whole. Fathers, you are to nurture (further the development of) their children. Your children cannot develop correctly without your attentive love and care. Fathers are to do it in the admonition (a gentle or friendly warning) of the Lord. God is the perfect example of a proper father. He is gentle and forgiving. Why, He even gave His precious son, Jesus, to save all of us from our lost state. Fathers, you wouldn't want to be the children of an uncaring, unloving, God, would you? The need, then, is for fathers to experience God's love for themselves and then love their children with the same wonderful unfailing love.

The significance of fathers loving their children is enormous. How can children respond to God, their spiritual father, if they know nothing of the love of their fathers? Fathers have been assigned by God the job of leader and head of the family unit. In this position, fathers can prepare their children to know the wonderful goodness of God by showing them what father love is. The opposite is also true. Fathers can harden their children's hearts to God by neglecting and rejecting their children. I know it is an awesome responsibility, but it is your duty as fathers. I repeat: You prepare your children's heart either to be open to the love of God, or to be hard and closed to it. Year after year, day after day, moment by moment of tuning out your children and their needs, of serving your own needs, of ignoring their cries for your love and affections, makes their hearts grow colder and harder. Their hearts become like rocks. And what can penetrate a rock? It is much easier to believe in something that you have seen than in something you have never seen. This is the significance of fathers loving their children: to teach them what being loved is like.

Not only are fathers not to provoke their children as mentioned above in Ephesians 6, but if we back up a few verses, we find this admonition:

> Children, obey your parents in the Lord: for this is
> right. Honor thy father and mother. Eph. 6:1-2

Imagine with me the insane paradox if this is expected out of children whose parents do not give them value and self-worth. Let me explain it this way: Fathers and mothers give birth to their children;

they have brought their children into the world. But then these parents do not give their children what they need to be whole and healthy: a proper self-image and acceptance. Oh, they feed them and educate them, but they never invest their time and effort in making sure their children know that they have value, are accepted and loved. The needs of their children's spirits are not meant. However, even after that kind of neglect, it is demanded that these children respect their parents. What would have to happen in children's minds for them to be able to do this? We would be asking them to do something irrational. We would be asking children to honor people who are holding the vital essentials they need to live, but are refusing to give. If someone had his or her hands tightly around our throat denying us the air we need to breathe, how much respect would we have for that person? Most likely, we would be kicking, screaming, and not showing respect for the person doing this to us. Who would simply lie there quietly and let this person cut off his or her air supply because of a compulsion for respect? Yet some parents give no mind or effort to their children's spiritual needs and then stand and demand those children respect them as their parents. It is insanity! Take your children in your arms over and over again and tell them you love them and then live a life that demonstrates that love. Granted, when parents are godly people who reflect the love of God by providing what children need, then the children are required by God to respect and honor them. Yet God does not like unjust scales:

> Dishonest scales are an abomination to the Lord, but a
> just weight is His delight. Prov. 11:1

Dishonest scales are where we cheat and give less than is required of us, but then stand and demand that we get all that we need and want.

All that we do for our children develops his or her heart into the kind of people they will be. Remember the scripture about the different kinds of ground seed can fall on? In Matthew 13:1-9, we read about the seed (the Word of God) being scattered. Some fell by the wayside (no soil), some fell on stony ground, some fell in thorns, and some fell on good ground. Only the seed that fell on good soil grew well and produced much fruit. We as parents have the task of taking our children's hearts and making them into good soil that will take in the word and love of God. If you are thinking that this task is just too difficult for you, know that this message is from God's Word; I am just agreeing with the Word and sharing the truth of it with you. Fathers (and mothers), loving your children will make them able to receive the Word of God into their hearts.

And Fathers, hear what God is specifically saying to you. Before Jesus came and ministered on this earth, God thought it was of the utmost importance that fathers return to loving their children again. There is an awesome call on your life from God. God the Father giving His own son to save His children is a perfect picture of the extent a father should go in loving and sacrificing for his children.

Jesus, when talking about the end times, said,

… the love of many shall wax cold. Matt. 24:12

We cannot let our love for our children grow cold. Christ is coming again to Earth, this time as the King of Heaven. God is sending out the call again, by the power of His Spirit. Prepare the way of the Lord, fathers, by loving your children.

Chapter 7

The Destruction of Me

It is said, "We came into this world with nothing and we will leave it the same way." This statement is not true. We came into this world with a physical body and a spirit, and we will leave this world with our spirit. This spiritual part of us will eternally exist. Parents start making deposits, either good or bad, into their children's spirits from day one. Each one of us then continues to make deposits into our own spirits all the days of our lives. If we think of our spirits as bank accounts, we know that anything that causes a negative balance is undesirable and has bad consequences.

This chapter is my personal story. It is how I came to understand the cry of the children from my own heart's cry, when I was a child. My heart hurt. I never understood the demands made on me to be normal even though I had no resources to meet those demands. I pray that my story helps someone somewhere understand life from a hurting child's point of view.

My Story

I love my family and thank God for them, but I must speak about the reality I experienced for the healing of myself and others. The truth sets us free, not a make-believe life in which we imagine that everything is fine so we can just survive.

My parents had some parenting skills that were wrong, but they had other skills that were very right. My dad taught me to love the truth above everything else. He never said it in exact, outright words, but stood firmly in the truth in everything he did. Anyone who knew him could see this in him. This path of healing is where the love of the truth led me. I honor my father in this journey. My earthly father led me to my Heavenly Father. The love of the truth he instilled in me provided a way for my salvation.

> … they received not the love of the truth, that they might be saved." II Thess. 2:10

My mother had a hunger to know God that inspired me to find God for myself. An important fact to mention here for all parents is that although my parents did some major things wrong, they showed me a path to God that I could follow. This one right way they practiced for me; they gave me the answer to all the other problems caused by them and the resulting hang-ups I acquired. No matter what wound I had, whether caused by them or my reaction to them, I found the answer for it in God. My parents gave me the most important thing needed: a way to God.

Please know, I fully understand that this is my perspective on my life. What else would I know? Other people who lived my life with me might see things from a different perspective, but this is the reality that I lived and the effect it had on me. I am hoping that I can help parents see life from the eyes of a needy child. Frequently, a parent or other adult's idea of what is happening totally differs from the way that a child perceives the situation. This would be a major objective of *The Cry of the Children*: to enable people who care for children to see from the child's concept of reality instead of their own. Only when we see the world through the children's eyes, where they are coming from, can we then go to them, take their hand, and bring them to the place they need to be. We will never reach the children or help them if we cannot first get to where they are.

My parents had five children. My mother had five pregnancies in five years. My brother was born first, healthy and strong. Next, my mother had two more sons who didn't survive because of a blood disorder called the RH factor. Then my sister came, and twelve months and twelve days later I arrived.

I truly do not know if my mother was trying to replace the sons she lost, but I was born at the end of a long, painful process and somehow developed the personality of needy. My mother was probably already worn out physically and emotionally. In any case, my earliest memories are of feeling unaccepted and being perceived as a bother. I annoyed my parents because I needed too much from them. My tenuous relationship with them left me feeling unfulfilled. Something was missing, and it was my self-esteem, my proper view of self. The needier I felt (my nickname was "Clutchy") and the more I tried to find acceptance, the more my parents pushed me away and the more unaccepted I felt. What was communicated to me very clearly was that it was not okay to be needy and because I was, I was not someone accepted by them. So, I was marked (or in biblical terms "cursed"): needy. This is where my hungry soul began. I was starving for someone to accept me. I worked very hard for many years of my life at finding acceptance, but I never really found it in any person.

Unfortunately, the stamp my parents marked me with stuck, and I subconsciously placed myself in the lives of people who agreed with it. After all, it was the identity they gave me. I didn't have any other identity. It was successfully communicated to my spirit that I was not accepted as part of the group of "normal" people (my family). What my parents dubbed (i.e., decided who I was) me, my sister, brother, and all the other relatives then accepted as my fate, the truth of who I really was. Their resulting attitude they had towards me was like a fence that kept me pinned into this train of thought and shaped my resulting behavior.

Do you recall the whole blessing and curse practice in the Bible, when the father laid his hands on the child and spoke a word from God over his or her life, and then that was the accepted path for the child? Everyone around this child then supported the pronouncement with their words and behavior towards that child. Well, this type of pronouncement still occurs today, though it is performed a little differently. We form an opinion of our children in our minds and then we speak and act in ways that agree with it. What's more, day in and day out, the message is heard by the children and others involved in his or her life. Then everyone goes along with what the person in authority says and makes it come true. I experienced the results of this. My parents pronounced over me, "needy," so that made me unaccepted, and my family members treated me accordingly. Of course, this pronouncement was never actually spoken, but it was communicated so that I believed it and everyone else accepted it as true, so it became my reality. If you tell children they are or aren't something, they will believe it. It is not easy to reveal one's life's problems to the world, but I know that I am not alone in my sorrow. There are many others who suffer the sadness of being branded in their youth as something negative and then being held captive there by their family. I, as a child, felt the pain of this inside. I was trying to live and find the value of my life and I was getting the message from those closest to me that I was defective and of no value. I speak the truth for all of us who have experienced this hardship. We parents need to see what is taking place and stop this negative practice.

Sadly, my parents had no idea that they had done this. They had no awareness that it had even came about. I am quite sure they did some wondering as to why I was so needy, though. Like many parents, they made no connection between my behavior and their behavior and attitude toward me. There was no understanding of the fact that we as parents tell the children who they are by our words and actions toward them. My parents, I am sure, simply thought that children become who they are all by themselves. Instead, I have lived with the stigma they actually gave me well into adulthood. The strange thing was that I never liked being what that stigma made me and I never stopped hating being treated as a needy person. It was terrible being this person.

Well, I had a child of my own one day, and can you guess how I treated him? I conveyed the same message to him that I had once been given: *You are bothersome, needy, and not accepted by me.* Only, because I had the wound of feeling unaccepted in me, I communicated even less acceptance to my son than my parents had to me. Well, it wasn't long before I saw the results of that parenting. I was shocked into waking up. My child was suffering my pain. This situation put me with my face on the floor, begging God for answers. I did not want my child to relive my horror. Inflicting the pain I knew so well on my kids was the point of my departure from that curse. Thus began my journey, and *The Cry of the Children* is the result of it.

What I want us to most to understand in this chapter is that our words, our attitude, and our actions towards our children tells him or her who they are. They will believe us. It will cement in their personalities and this is who they will become. Also, those around them in the family will all play along with what we, the parents, decide and speak. If we communicate to our children that they are defective in some way, then that is how they will view themselves and that is how others, especially other children in the family who respect our opinion, will view them. Do we realize how hard it is for children with their limited knowledge of who they are not to succumb to that curse? Thankfully, as an adult I found my acceptance and value in a relationship with God, realizing that:

> When my father and my mother forsake me, then the
> Lord will take me up. Ps. 27:10

The most bothersome thing to me, though, is the fact that after years of changing and building my true identity as a valuable person and living it out before people, many members of my family still see me in the same light in which my parents painted me. No matter what I do, say, or have become, they hold on to the old view of me. If that isn't a curse, I don't know what is. This stubborn way of thinking is tantamount to one's relatives keeping you in a prison. I can be this new person I have become and then be around a family member that views me the old way, and the former view has a power that takes control of me. I start falling into the old way of thinking and behavior. It is a real battle of the mind and heart. I say all this to illustrate how hard it is for a person to overcome a negative picture of himself or herself that has been imparted during his or her childhood, so parents can be alerted to the handicap it gives a child. This is precisely why we, as parents, must be constantly aware of what we are declaring to our children about who they are. It takes a conscious effort to stay positive. It takes communicating good things no matter how we feel and no matter how good or bad the child has been. We will want to make up our minds about what we want to communicate to our children and make our words, attitude, and actions line up with it. Too often we let our mood or how we feel physically dictate what we communicate to our children.

I want to honor my parents by acknowledging that they did everything they knew and understood to be right. They were working from the faulty structure that they were given by their own parents. If I were to have a condemning attitude toward my mother and father for their bad parenting, then I too would need to be condemned for the same reason. That's why I want to repeat that the point they really got right was to give me a way to God, because this is the path through which I found my answers. Parents, you can get many things wrong, but get this right: Give your child a road to God and they will find the healing and restoration that they need for all the things that go awry in life. I am not giving you an excuse to continue the way you are if you find that you are parenting wrong. I am, however, giving you a point of grace to keep you while you change into what you should be. I'm on this road with you, praying that God will have mercy on all of us as we begin the process of hearing and responding to the cry of our children.

Chapter 8

Loving the Little Children

I remember being in high school and reading a book about a man who injected himself with some kind of dye to make his skin dark so that he could live amongst the black people. It was during the time in our nation when African Americans were not afforded equality. This man wanted to live as a black man so that he could understand how blacks were treated and how it felt to live without rights. It cost him a great deal to identify with this group of people, but he learned exactly what their life was like. He experienced a life he never would have known as a white person in our country, during that time period.

Similarly, if we are going to understand our children and what their needs are, we must identify with life from their point of view. We certainly cannot shrink ourselves back into children, but what we can do is shut off our adult reasoning, humble ourselves, and put ourselves mentally in the position of a child. We will never understand what children need until we are able to see life from their point of view.

In order to comprehend life as a child, stop talking and become a quiet observer. Perhaps some of us have the wrong idea of how to connect with our children. I know I did. No one learns anything about anybody when all that occurs is a person running around giving orders and making demands. Try to sit quietly and watch your child in their life situations. When my grandchildren come to visit, they will sit for long periods of time playing with the toys I have put out for them. I just sit and listen to them while they play. I have learned a lot about their personalities by listening to them play-act with their toys. I listen and I plant in my memory what they talk about. When the opportunity arises and when it is relevant, I bring up something they have said in the past while playing. When I do this, they stop and look at me, and their eyes will get really big. The message comes across loud and clear: "I am *important to you*, you pay attention to what I say and do, and you remember it." There is so much to learn about our children, if we would just be quiet enough so they can teach us. We will have to get the idea out of our heads that we are to be constantly instructing them and instead let them teach us about themselves.

Children want to be heard and understood. When they are, it gives them value, a sense of belonging in the families and societies in which they live. I have taught groups of children for years, and I have learned that one of the things they love most is to be heard. If I would ask a question in a group of children that required them to tell something about themselves, I would always have more hands up than time available to take answers. They all wanted to be heard, even the kids who were normally very quiet. It means the world to children. Their little spirits receive the message, *I'm important; I've been heard.* Children understand the importance of someone hearing them even if we adults have forgotten how to listen. If we listen, our children will tell us what they need. Remember that God said,

… and a little child shall lead them. Isa. 11:6

God also said we have to become like little children to enter the kingdom of heaven (Matt. 18:3). So, you see, we can learn a lot from children.

Children not only need to be heard and what they say acknowledged; they also need to be seen. This requires eye contact. In order to do this, we adults have to slow down, take our focus off of other things, and put our attention on our children. We need to physically get down on the children's level and look them in the eye when we talk with them. It speaks volumes to children about how much we care for them. When we look someone in the eye as we are talking to them, we are saying, "I am focusing on you because you matter." We do not only need to do this with our kids, but with all of the people in our lives. Honestly, I am terrible at this when it comes to the adults in my life. When I ask myself why, I realize that it is because I do not want to connect with people; I have too many other things on my mind. I use the excuse that I am just too busy. Isn't this a typical, modern adult, American trait? This is what we have evolved to in our fast-paced lives, but it isn't good. When we do look our children in the eye as we are talking with them, we are making a connection with them. This connection is absolutely essential if they are to understand that they have value to us and they have value in this world.

Touch is another way to communicate love and value to our children. I have raised four children and now have four grandchildren. For all of you parents and grandparents who can identify with me, I don't have to tell you that life does not slow down when your children leave home and start their own families. You just shift into high gear, especially during holidays. My hands have been very busy for many years in the caring of my family. It is amazing how much work you can ask your hands to do without wearing them out. Thank God for that. When I think of how much work my hands have done compared to how many times I have reached out to tenderly touch my children or grandchildren, though, I am ashamed. I know for a fact that the thing they will remember is not all the work, but the times I reached out to them and touched them–giving my son a pat on the back when I was proud of him, giving my daughter a hug when she was sad about something, taking my granddaughter's hand and pulling her up the hill during a family hike, or stroking my grandchild's head when she shared something important to her. To reach out and touch someone is to say, "I care about you." We parents and grandparents need to stop what we are so busy with and reach out a kind hand more often to the ones we love.

43

Our children are not stupid. They hear what we communicate to them very clearly. If we do not listen to them, understanding what they are saying or where they are coming from, our children will get the message, *I am not important enough for my parents to take the time to know me.* When we cannot even stop and focus on them when we talk with them, they will certainly understand, *I just take up my parents' time and bother them.* If we cannot reach out and touch our children with tenderness, but do not hesitate to use our hands to discipline them, they certainly get the message, *I don't deserve kindness.* Children are good students of what we are teaching them. We parents are the ones not getting the facts. If we are communicating non-value, then our children will not value themselves. This can create many miserable human beings.

Hearing our children, seeing them, and touching them in caring, positive ways are all means by which we can build value in their spirits, value that nothing can ever remove. It will be like a stone wall that negativity cannot penetrate. It only costs us time and attention. Those are two very valuable things that we should be spending on human lives, not on material objects or jobs–especially on the human lives that we brought into this world and call our family.

Chapter 9

Letting Your Child Teach You

In the lives we live, we clearly understand the fact that when something we depend on does not function properly we need to find out what is wrong with it and do what is necessary to fix it. If we don't, the problem will get worse and eventually the thing on which we depend will break down and fail us completely.

We have two shared cars in our family. I usually drive the smaller one because I like the fact that I can get into small parking spaces if necessary. One day I was driving the larger vehicle and I heard a grinding noise. I went home and told another family member who usually drives this car. This person plays the radio frequently, so the noise probably went unnoticed. Sure enough, when checked out, there was a brake problem. I shudder to think of the brakes failing on some of the mountains through which we drive. If we don't listen to our brakes when they start squealing, we are in for a more costly repair bill or a dangerous driving incident. We can rely on the same common sense in our parenting skills. If life is not functioning in the realm of what we call normal (healthy, productive, positive) for our children, then we can be sure something needs to be looked at and fixed in our family life.

When our children misbehave, it can be the warning sign telling us that there is a problem. I have come to understand that if we parents are faltering in a particular area of parenting, our children will be a constant irritant to us because they will be suffering from this place of lack and making it known to us through wrong behavior. In my life, I annoyed my parents because I needed something more from them. This very annoyance was actually pointing out to them that they had a problem in their parenting. They had no idea that their most important priority as a parent was to make sure their children knew they were loved and accepted by them, therefore creating the healthy self-worth that every child needs as a foundation for a healthy personality. It is my impression that my parents' generation was more concerned with their children becoming too prideful than they were with children having healthy self-esteem. I was not receiving love and acceptance from my parents. Through my behavior I was telling my parents loudly and clearly that I needed something more. They, however, did not understand the message. If they had viewed it the right way, they could have identified the problem and corrected it. This would have benefited all the children in the family, because we all grew up with problems that stemmed from this evident deficiency to which I was reacting. Instead, my parents viewed me as having a problem and branded me "needy." In contrast, we parents need to respond to the problems we are having with our children as if they are alarms telling us our parenting needs correcting somewhere. We have to search out the problems until we can put a finger on what they are. It will take some serious soul searching before God, but it will be worth it. If we continue to blame the child, we will go uncorrected and wound all our children with the fault in us. While we are pointing a finger at our children and finding fault with their behavior, more fingers will be pointing back at us as the problem–but unfortunately, we all too often won't even see them, instead continuing to be blind to the true source of these problems.

When it came to my own children, I started out reacting to their bad behavior the same way my parents did to mine. When I saw my parent/child relationship only getting worse and heading for destruction, I asked God to show me the answer. I learned that our children will tell us what we are doing wrong if we will listen to them, and I also learned that God will tell us what we need to do to fix it if we will ask for His help. With God's help, I worked on correcting my parenting. It was not an easy task, but I saw amazing results in my children when I let them teach me through their behavior where I was failing as a parent. I am convinced that after generations of my family not tending to our children's spirits and not dealing with the children's problems constructively, my children would have been greatly impaired in life if changes were not made. My first child taught me so much about my bad parenting, while my three younger children should be very thankful to their sibling because they reaped great benefits from what I learned and corrected in my parenting skills. It sounds so easy, written down in this chapter, but it involved taking my personality apart and fixing the broken pieces. Although the results are worth it, I am still doing the repair work. That is why I hope you will trust me and get started on your own repair work right away, if it is needed.

Chapter 10

Protecting Your Child's Spirit

What would we say if the President of the United States held a press conference and announced to the country he was disbanding the United States Military: the Army, Navy, Marine Corps, Air Force, and Coast Guard? We would all be frantic to stop him, probably by impeachment. Then we would put a new person in the position, someone who cared about protecting our nation. And so the question arises: Given that we, as parents, are the leaders of our families, how good of a job are we doing protecting them? If we aren't doing the job, then who is?

In this chapter, we need to consider why we need to protect our children's spirits from destruction, and how. Do we know what the enemies of our children's spirits are? Time, energy, and resources need be spent researching how we can best protect the children. We parents are the Homeland Security for our children and our families. If we haven't filled this position, then I dare to tell you the truth: Our children and families are unprotected and the enemy will come into our home to destroy them.

Are you familiar with the second law of thermodynamics, which describes basic principles familiar in everyday life? It is partially a universal law that states that everything ultimately falls apart and disintegrates over time unless acted on by another force. Therefore, anything left unattended and uncared for will automatically be subject to decay. Consider the places we live: If we do nothing to them, don't clean them, repair them, or keep them up, they will decay and fall apart. The same is true of our families and children. We do not seem to fully understand this concept when it applies to people. Most of us completely understand this law when we think of our physical homes, but do not apply it when it comes to the care of people in our lives. Many of us are very attentive to seeing that a leaky roof or broken furnace is repaired, but when it comes to the concept of protective knowledge for the upkeep of children's or families' spiritual well-being, we do not even know the elementary, essential concepts.

The most obvious way to protect our children's spirits is to be on the lookout for problems, anything not functioning properly. Is that not what we do with our homes? If the home is cold in the winter, then we know that something is wrong with the furnace. Anything not commonly accepted as normal behavior in children will signal that something dangerous to our children's spirits exists. If we are not alert when a suspicious behavior appears and it goes ignored for a while, we face the danger of it becoming deeply engrained into our children's personalities. Then we are in for a real battle. It is better to be like the people of old who lived in walled cities. They set watchmen on the walls as lookouts for any coming danger. The watchmen would yell, ring a bell, or use whatever means they could to warn everyone in the city when they saw danger, and in response, the people scrambled to prepare to defend their city. In the same way, we need to pay close attention and respond promptly to any and all signs of danger.

Speaking of walls, are there walls surrounding our children? What would form a spiritual wall of protection around our children, protecting their spirits? Well, one spiritual thing we can do to build this wall is pray for our children, morning, noon, and night. We should pray the Word of God over them. We should get a word from God for them, and then believe it, speak it, and stand on it, especially, when the opposite behavior is staring us right in the face. We can start with this scripture in the Psalms,

> Lo, children are a heritage of the Lord: and the fruit of the womb is his reward. As arrows are in the hand of a mighty man; so are children of the youth. Happy is the man that hath his quiver full of them: they shall not be ashamed, but they shall speak with the enemies in the gate. Ps. 127: 3-5

The devil should not be allowed to use our children to make our lives miserable; instead, our children should figuratively be the arrows we shoot at him.

Remember, to win a battle, we must fight a war. We can go to prayer for our children and fight for their souls. We have to get mad at the enemy and fight for our children in the spirit (engaging in spiritual battle by praying and standing on the Word of God). Let us put our foot down and tell the enemy to get out of our homes and our families. If we are having a problem with our children, we can pray and ask God for wisdom (James 1:5). We can be courageous in the battle for our children's spirits and trust that God will give us creative ideas that work to fix our problems. We are encouraged,

> Only be thou strong and very courageous … Josh. 1:7

That's what God told Joshua (four times in Chapter 1) when Joshua was going to battle for a place for his people to possess. Similarly, we need to courageously fight for a good, safe place where our children's spirits can exist.

One last analogy might prove helpful here. If we found out there were termites in our house, what would we do? Would we continue to live in that house and ignore them? No, we would go call an exterminator immediately. Likewise, after we become aware that our children have a problem, we need to immediately set ourselves to resolving the problem, regardless of the cost or effort on our part. We must put all our effort into finding an answer. God says that if we seek, we will find, if we ask, it will be given, and if we knock, the door will be opened (Matt. 7:7). We can go searching for our answers knowing we will find them. We should never give up until we find the answers we need. We can know that God is with us in this and that He will help us (Gal. 13:5-6).

Another element that will build a wall of protection around your children is love. Remember,

Love never fails … 1 Cor. 13:8

It will help to read all of 1 Cor. 13 several times, until having a deep understanding of love, and then attempt to love our children.

The following is my parental interpretation of that chapter:

1. Love is patient. We need to take a big dose of patience now because we are going to need it for all the spilled milk, endless questions, repeated commands, and many other trying situations throughout our children's lives. Always bear in mind that in every situation our children face, we are either communicating to him or her, "I love you" or "You are a big annoyance."

2. Love is kind, the opposite of mean. We know how easy it is to fall into being mean when we lack #1 (patience).

3. Love is not proud. It is not about big, old us; it is about these precious little children asking us in one hundred different ways and for the one hundredth time, "What is my value?" We need to get big old us out of the way and love our children.

4. Love does not behave in an unseemly manner. Far too many of us have behaved so unseemly when we've reached the end of #1 (patience) with our children. I am ashamed to say that I have. Admit the truth and stop the behavior.

5. Love is not easily provoked. This is a difficult area for me. When I was in my wounded state, I sometimes would take offense at anything and everything. Taking care of our own wounds in our spirits is important because if we fail to do this, we can become

short-tempered with our children. Does flying off the handle at every little thing communicate love to our children? No, it says, "You are a pest, a problem, a menace to my life." Remember, we are telling them who they are. They will believe us.

6. Love thinks no evil. If we fall into the trap of thinking that our children are evil, they will catch on and live up to that. I am not referring to the fact that we all have sinful natures and therefore do evil (Rom. 3:23). I am talking about children to whom we are communicating what his or her core value is. If our children think that we, their parents, think they are evil, where are they supposed to go from there? There is no real hope in that situation for our children. The children's actions may be evil but they must be loved–always. Love them in the same way that God loves us: unconditionally.

7. Love rejoices not in wrong but rejoices in truth. We cannot let our guard down and just accept bad behavior; it should always have a consequence. But at the same time, separate the behavior from the children that we love. We must keep communicating to our children that our love will never go away or change. God loves us even when we are in our worst, most sinful state. He loves us in that state until the day we die. Shouldn't our children know and experience that same truth from us? If our so-called love for them is dependent upon their behavior, it is not love at all, because love never fails (#11).

8. Love bears all things. No matter how difficult the going gets, love bears it and keeps on loving. We cannot let anything compromise our love for our children. We should learn this early because we will need that love to be strong, especially when our children become teenagers and we no longer have any intelligence in his or her eyes. Any mother of a teenage daughter understands what I am talking about. If we enter our children's teenage years with a wound still in our spirit, I guarantee you, we are going to react wrongly to their attack on our character. It takes a strong, whole person to stand up to a teenager's natural rejection of us, the parents, as he or she tries

to figure out who they are on the way to independent adulthood. Bear it and love them through it.

9. Love hopes all things. What do we hope for our children? Convene with God and find out. We should write down our hopes for our children, reread them daily, and memorize them. We should commit these hopes to God ("Commit thy way unto the Lord; trust also in Him and He shall bring it to pass," Ps. 37:5.) Remember, hope is belief in what we can't see yet. Keep that in mind when we interact with our children. Even though we cannot always see good results right away, keep hoping for and believing in those hopes.

10. Love endures all things. In view of this verse, we know we can't give up and treat our children with disrespect when we feel we can't take it anymore. Instead, we need to push through adversity and communicate, "I love you."

11. Love never fails. Those words alone tell us that we will never fail as a parent if we love our children. No matter how many times we figuratively drop love, we have to pick it up again and hold it tight. The fact that we will drop love is a known, but the day we fail to bend down and pick it back up again is the day we will really fail and guarantee the failure of our children. We need to look for ways to show them our love. We don't only do things we want to do with our children, but things they would like to do. We need to get beside our children and get to know them well.

In sum, recognize that we are the only protection our children and family have. We need be alert to problems and do something about these problems when we see them. By doing these things, we will be giving love to our children. That sounds very elementary, but it's not always easy to practice. We should take seriously the protection of our children's eternal spirits. If we turn our hearts towards our children, all of our resources will be used to care for them.

Chapter 11

Who's to Blame?

I saw in the news a story of a boy who was bullied and beat up by five or six other boys much bigger than him. Someone had recorded the whole long incident on a cell phone. The bullies ended the horrid abuse with hanging their victim up on a fence by his coat. Then the news report showed the police had caught the boys responsible and were leading them away in handcuffs. Most people viewing the episode would feel the situation was dealt with properly.

We all pride ourselves in our zero tolerance for bulling in our schools and communities. We feel satisfied when the bully is caught and punished.

But do we ever stop and consider what makes a child a bully? I think we would all agree that children figuratively are little copy machines. They watch and then imitate what they have seen. However, the information the children pick up and deposit in their intellect doesn't always come out the way it went in. We adults demonstrate our attitudes and mindsets via the actions we perform in front of our kids. They observe us. Our behaviors are processed through their hearts and minds, and their interpretation shows up in the way they handle different situations in their lives. We adults can be communicating things to our children by our behavior and have no idea what we are telling them. I would say that 95% of the time I could trace my children's bad behavior back to some bad behavior of mine that I was totally blind to at the time. What the child is doing is not always easy to interpret, but if you are honest with yourself, you will see the connection between their behavior and what you have conveyed, even if not in words. Children are pretty much blank slates at the time of birth. We start writing on them as soon as we take them in our arms and look them in the eyes.

The problem is, most of the time, we fail to make the connection between what we are doing in front of our children and what they then repeat back to us in their behavior. Bullying, for example, does not simply just occur for no reason. It has many sources in our society today. Intolerance for people different from us is one of the sources. Mockery, I have noticed, is rampant today, and shows intolerance. Mockery occurs when: looking at someone with a critical attitude and then voicing our disapproval in a degrading or comical way. Adults practice it every day. We might say, "Oh, we don't do that." I bet if we put a mockery alarm on us, though, we would be surprised how many times it would go off in a day's time. Teens have mastered the gift of mockery to the extreme. It seems to be their favorite pastime. Many current situation comedy TV shows constantly demonstrate behavior that is unkind to others as being amusing and acceptable. I would call this the seed that is planted in a heart that could bloom into a bully, wouldn't you? I don't know if I heard this somewhere or came up with it myself, but it certainly fits what some bullies could say to their parents: "You have made me what I am, but you hate what I have become."

In my experience with my children, when they were a victim of a bully, it occurred in an environment in which the adults were playing favorites with kids. Certain kids were untouchable because of various reasons (parents having money or position, for example) and they were therefore allowed to treat others as they pleased. Bullying was running wild. Who's to blame? I would blame the adults in charge. I fear this is the case in many bullying situations. Certain adults have somehow communicated the message, "All clear for bullying" and kids have picked it up and run with it. But who does the hammer come down on when the bullying is brought to light? Why, the wicked children who did it, of course, or, sometimes, the children who react negatively to it. So many times, in the name of discipline, the children reap the horrid outcome for the behavior that we adults have taught them. We fail to see that the root of the behavior is in us.

This is why all the anti-bullying posters I see in schools upset me. Isn't that just like us to put up posters, have campaigns, hold assemblies and invite special speakers, have documentaries on TV, and on and on, without looking back and finding out where this ugly thing grew from? Who planted it? Who watered it? What allowed it to grow?

Consider the best way to handle problems that arise when gardening. When we pull out a weed in our garden so our tomatoes will grow, do we pull the weed off at the surface of the ground? No, because it will just grow back and we will have to pull it again. Instead, we take our shovel, if necessary, and dig that unwanted thing out by its roots. Where is this same wisdom when we need to know what to do when our children have a problem? Because we are embarrassed at the reflection on us, we tend to dole out an overly aggressive punishment to our children, with lots of verbal instruction to boot, and let the matter go at that, never looking back. And then we are oh-so-surprised when the behavior comes back again. But did we take the time to dig up the cause? No, we did not. Doing this would require time, energy, and reflection we were not willing to give the situation. Take notice how we only give the valuable assets of time, energy, and thought to what we really value in life.

Bullying is a result of our society's sad social skills, which our children have picked up very well and are demonstrating before our very eyes. We don't like what we see. It is ugly! Will it make us search for the source of this evil destructive behavior? More often than not, we just make the bullies out to be terrible criminals and hang another poster saying, "Zero tolerance for bullying." What is the next ugly thing we are going to teach our kids? We have gone from a twelve-year run of school shootings to rampant bullying problems that have caused child suicides. God help us, what is next?

I would rather look into myself and see where I have failed then continue this downward spiral of destructive behavior. Will you please join me? It is a difficult task, as it involves changing ourselves (probably the hardest known thing for humans to do, which is why we need God) but, it is still an easier path than this long road. What led me to realize this? Loving my children and seeing the pain they were suffering. I would have ripped out my heart and asked for a new one if I could change what was in me that was bringing destruction to my child. Actually, I did do that spiritually. Actually, God did it in me–and He continues to do it. It seems to be a lifelong process (Ezek. 11:19-20). If we don't let God do this, we will live with the results of the evil we have stored up in our hearts and passed down to our children like a bad inheritance.

Love the children. Hate the bad examples we are, but please, love the children.

Chapter 12

Helping a Child with a Wounded Spirit

In the past, I had caused damage to my children's spirits before I realized what I was doing. I wounded my children's spirits by not communicating effectively to them that they had value and that I accepted them. Instead, I succeeded in making my children believe that they had a problem and I did not accept them because of it. That set the scene for my children to act out destructively. Then this behavior only led to more feedback from me with the same negative message: rejection. We were caught in a trap. This situation created a very bad environment for my children in which to experience life.

My children's experience was a repeat of my childhood, only I seemed so much better at communicating the wrong ideas to my children than my parents had been. The old saying, "What the parents are in moderation the children will be in excess" proved very true. However, I could see the harm being done to my children's spirits, while my parents never understood the damage that was done to mine.

As I stated earlier, I went to God for all my answers. In the rest of this chapter, I would like to just share some tidbits of wisdom God gave me along the way. Some of these thoughts I have mentioned previously, but I would like to restate again. Sometimes it helps to read information again, stated in a different way, as doing so causes the light of understanding to turn on. The important thing is that our children receive all the proper assistance they need from us.

1. When you have a child who has times of extreme anger or uncontrolled behavior, learn to deal with those times in faith, not fear. Fear will cause you to react wrongly and as a result cause more damage. Don't view this situation from the perspective of a victim caught in a bad circumstance. Look at it from the positive position of, "I am going to find an answer to this problem" and "God says he will never leave me and that he is my helper" (Heb. 13: 5-6).

2. Learn the difference between acting in the flesh (through human reasoning or intellect) and acting in the spirit (from our spirit, where the Holy Spirit comes to dwell with us and guide us). The Bible tells us that acts in the flesh bring death, whereas acts in the spirit bring life (Rom. 8:13). We have all, at one time or another, brought death to our relationships with our children through reacting to them in our flesh. The love that our children will respond to comes from our hearts, where our spirits reside. It is encouraging to know that we can bring life again by living from our spirit and acting in the Holy Spirit's power. When we are in the spirit, we can minister to our children's spirits.

3. Understand that our own spirits need care. God made the spirit place in us so we can commune with Him, who is spirit, and have a relationship with Him, knowing Him intimately. To do this, we can pray, read the Bible, seek God's face, and receive life from Him through belief in Jesus Christ, His son. Jesus said that He is life and that He came to give us abundant life (John 10:10). We cannot give life to anyone else unless we have life. I don't mean to oversimplify this part. My life in God is the reason why I found my answers. I have seen many other lives shipwrecked and ruined

because people didn't know where to turn for answers. Life in God is just that: LIFE. (Chapter 13 contains more details on how to have a relationship with God.)

4. Happy, well-adjusted children come from happy, well-adjusted parents. If our spirits exist in wounded states because of negative forces that have come against their well-being and damaged them, we will pass our wounds along to our children, plus a few extra ones. We will be inflicting wounds on our children in the areas in which we lack healing. My mother, whose mother never communicated to her that she was valuable, failed to communicate to me the fact that I was a valuable person. Consequently, I felt invisible and worthless. Then, as an adult, I battled daily with self-worth. While I struggled, I could not communicate to my children that they were valuable to me because I didn't know my own value. I was often miserable in my struggle and became negative and critical of my children, adding wound upon wound. The generations of wounds pile up and grow into a miserable existence for everyone involved. Each wounded person adds to the cycle, passing on the wound to the next generation without ever dealing with it. We can change this destructive interaction and make it stop. We can find healing for the wounds in our spirits and turn down a whole new road for our lives, our children's lives, and all the generations to come. We can end the hurt, sorrow, and pain. It involves healing and walking in a better way. We will have to choose life and give up all the deathly practices we have learned. We will have to start caring about our spirits and what's going on in them. Only then can we minister what is needed to our children's spirits.

5. To restate the unwritten law at work here, what the parent is, the child will be, only multiplied by ten times or more, good or bad. We must understand and remember this fact. What spoke volumes to me was when I observed other parents who did well with their children and then saw the effect I had on my children. A kind parent produces an even kinder child. An angry, impatient parent produces an even more angry and impatient child. Harshness is

a parental habit I have noticed that is so obvious when passed on to children. The flip-side is gentleness. These two qualities can be communicated in so many ways: words, touch, reaction, and facial expressions. Gentleness and harshness are two things that speak volumes. They say, "I have all the time in the world for you" or "You really are hard to deal with." Gentleness is very hard to master for those who do not obtain it from their parents. But the quality of gentleness makes all the difference in how your child will deal with everything and everybody in his or her life. From the time that we first handle our newborn child to wiping our toddler's face and speaking to our teenager, gentleness speaks our heart to our children. We either react in harsh or gentle ways, in so doing, teaching our children's spirits to do the same. A child who is tossed about as a baby, grabbed as a toddler, yelled at as a teen, and exposed to a myriad of other harsh reactions from his parent will in turn react with harshness to what comes his or her way in life. Harshness has been taught to them, and it has taken firm root in their spirit. It is what they have known. Handling a child with harshness says to him or her, "You are not important enough for me to take the time to handle you with care." In contrast, a child who is handled gently with tender hands when bathed, a toddler who is given a gentle hand to lead it out of danger, a teen who is approached with a gentle voice of reason and instruction will deal with his or her world with a gentle spirit. If children are handled in gentleness, this is what their spirits know and what they will display to others. Gentleness brings the traits of love, care, and value to our children's spirits. Taking time and being patient with our children will tell them, "You are a treasure to me."

6. We must never, never, never give up on our children. Hopelessness is the number one tool the Devil uses in his attempt to destroy our children. He uses it every day to beat down the child's sense of security. Children's hope is fragile while they are growing up, especially until they have enough positive things in their lives to strengthen themselves in spirit. We parents have to build our

children a foundation of hope in their spirits. If we who gave our children physical life give up on our children, who on this earth is there left to fight off the enemy of their souls? If we give up, our children will understand this to mean they are hopeless. Hopeless people do the most evil things this world has ever heard of. They are people who have been convinced that they have no worth or value. They can be the angriest souls alive. People without hope want to hurt other people because they have the life which was denied them. They want to take that life away from others. Valuable life was withheld from them, so why should others be allowed to enjoy it? When dealing with our children and their problems, we should always believe that God will give us the answers we need. Never accept anything else. We must be more persistent in hope than our children are in bad behavior. Forgive, be kind, and offer grace. We should offer our children as much grace as God has offered us. In case we have forgotten exactly what grace God has given us, remember that He forgives all our sins, heals us, keeps us, accepts us into His beloved family, and satisfies us with good things (Ps. 103:1-5 and Ps. 68:19).

7. Truth is the surest path to lead our children to God. We should be teaching our children to live truthfully. Do not just demand conformity to our standards and accept that as mission accomplished when it is done. Underneath could be laying the same problem waiting to come out in another behavior. Conformity to our set of rules is not the goal, living honestly is. Let us ask ourselves this; Would we rather have children who fake it and behave just to make us happy and get what they want, or children who behave because they want to be good? One of these is what we might call a hypocrite. That child will grow up to be exactly what he was hiding under the surface of fake behavior all along. Teaching our children to live honestly from their spirits is what is essential. If the behavior is bad, then at least we know what we are dealing with now while they are young, and we can do something about it. If we teach our children to be hypocrites, just acting out a fake

existence their whole childhood, when they grow up and go out to live their lives on their own, the facade will come off. What are we going to do about the problem then? There is not much we can do by the time our children are adults, except be there for them when they have to deal with the bad situations they make for themselves.

8. If our children do not get what they need from us, they will become self-centered and go looking for it elsewhere. When we do not meet the needs of our children's spirits to be accepted, loved, and appreciated, they find a way to fill the need themselves. Then we wonder why our children are so self-centered. Nobody else has communicated true care and concern for who they are or what they want, so to preserve mental health they take over the job. What else can they do: just become nonexistent in their spirit? If we tried to exist with no spirit, what kind of people would we be? We can no more deny our spirits than we can deny our bodies or brains. The problem with the self-centeredness that is created is that it is the opposite of what a well-adjusted person should be, especially someone called a Christian. Also, this self-centeredness leads our children to satisfy themselves with things that are substitutes for what is truly needed. These substitutes are just that, something else used because the real thing is not available. In my life, I needed to have the good and wonderful experience of knowing that I was loved and accepted as a child. I did not have this experience, so I took over the job at which my parents failed. If they were not going to give me something good that I needed, then I would find something good to give myself. That something good I substituted for love and acceptance was food. Thus began my years of struggle with eating. I longed for good to be given to me, my parents failed to give me this good in its proper form, and so I gave it to myself in another form, food. Good, in its real form of the love and acceptance I needed, would have given me life; the substitute has brought me nothing but misery and further destruction to my self-esteem. Controlling my eating habits has been an ongoing problem in my

life. When you, as an adult, try to rip out of you the thing you have depended on for good in your life, since you were a child, it is far from easy. Thankfully, I found out that God had an answer for this problem. God assured me that when my parents neglected me, then He would pick me up and love me (Ps. 27:10). God gave me the love and acceptance I needed. He satisfied my heart with all the good things for which it longed (Ps. 103:5). I hope that this personal illustration shows why we parents should be the ones to give our children what they need. If we don't, we are just signing them up for many other hang-ups that will complicate their lives. Living in this world is difficult enough; we do not need to make it worse for our children by denying them what they need from us. They are not qualified to make wise choices in filling their own needs.

9. We should not make the mistake of thinking that giving our children religion is giving them God, religion being defined as keeping a set of dos and don'ts, attending church for social status, putting on the appearance of good behavior, and speaking all the correct religious jargon. Religion does not tend to the needs of our children's spirits. Religion deadens the spirit. Only a relationship with God through Jesus Christ gives life to the spirit. It is this relationship with God that changes our hearts from evil to good because of who we love. It is real, from the heart, rather than a matter of the outward appearance. The best thing we can do is find this experience and live it out in front of our children, showing them that it is possible.

10. Pay close attention: When we see early signs of something wrong in our children's personalities, begin immediately planning for its exit. Do not ever accept a bad habit and let it take root in your children's personalities. Pray and ask God for His wisdom in dealing with it. Whoever or whatever is more persistent is the one who wins, either the bad habit or us saying it has to go. Persistence in prayer can make many a bad habit disappear from our children's personalities.

11. It is important to understand, in reference to our children's ability to learn mentally and mature socially, that if their spirit is wounded they will be handicapped in those two areas. Even though I passed

every grade in school, I did not learn well. I simply did not have the mental capacity to process information and retain it. Upon reaching adulthood and receiving ample healing of my spirit, I had no difficulty in learning. As I look back on my childhood and my lack in this area, it seems I was in a mental fog. The fog was my terrible self-esteem. It put my mind in such a state that I could not learn properly. The amazing thing to me was seeing how well I could learn once I no longer had issues with self-esteem. One cannot teach a wounded creature anything. It is too busy dealing with its pain. This is another area in which we make demands on our children that cannot come to fruition due to what has been given to our children or denied them.

12. A word about using threats when dealing with our children: In Ephesians 6:9, we read that masters are not to use threats when dealing with those under them. I think that this is very good advice for parents, too. When we use threats to get our children to do what we want, we are not fostering honest behavior. In contrast, we are teaching our children to behave only because we are watching them and liable to carry out a threat. Of course many of us do not follow through on what we say, and we consequently lose credibility with our children. It would be much better to instill intrinsic motivation in our children. If they learn to behave only because someone is standing over them with threats and not because they want to do the right thing, what kind of people will they be as adults? Is a person who only does the right thing when someone is watching a good citizen? No, and that is why we are admonished in Ephesians 6:6 not to do our work for the approval of men but to do all things as to the Lord, from our hearts. After providing instruction, we need to allow our children to choose their behavior, with no threats involved. For example, instead of making the threat, "If you don't make your bed you will not get to go outside and play," simply ask the child to make his bed. If he chooses not to do it, the next time he asks for something from you, say, "No; you did not make your bed when I asked you to." The child then learns that if he does not

listen and do what he is told to do, an unpleasant consequence will result. He learns to choose right behavior because it is good for him, not because someone is watching over him and going to make him pay if he does wrong. These two circumstances sound similar, but they are not. One child will grow up learning to do the right thing because someone is watching, while the other one will do the right thing because he knows that it is good for him. Teaching our children to learn to choose right behavior honestly from their hearts is more beneficial than teaching them to choose it because of others power or control over them.

13. Making changes in our lives and in how we do things can be extremely difficult. If we behave a certain way for a long time and then want to change and behave differently, not everyone around us will want to change along with us, especially our children. Making changes in the wrong way can bring about disturbing reactions from others that make us want to go running back to our old behavior like it is a long-lost friend. However, this impulse only takes us back to where we started. Understand that just because we see the truth and want to walk in a different direction does not mean that everyone else will be willing to walk there with us. When we make changes in the ways in which we deal with our children, we have to be ready for the backlash, or even the whiplash. When we encounter bad reactions, we have to understand that it is not to be punished as disobedience. We have done something the wrong way for a long time and we have created a life with our children supporting this way of interacting together. We need to really comprehend this fact and be willing to take the time it may take to correct it. We should make the changes necessary, and then give our children the space they need to adjust. Also, we need to accept the truth that we created this whole reality to start with, rather than taking out our frustration (over the work it takes to fix it) on our children. Everything we do reaps results, and when we've done something over and over for years, we have created a negative environment for us and our children around the situation. This is the reality our children know and operate

in, right or wrong. When we make a change, our children have to adjust, and that takes time. Look at what I am saying this way: We had a bad way of dealing with our children. Our children then acquired their own bad way of reacting as a result of that. Now we have corrected our problems, but our children still practice the bad behavior they learned. Their way of reacting has taken up residence in their personalities. Do we, as the creator of this problem, have a right to come down hard on our children for this behavior? No. We need to offer our children repeated grace and mercy until they can come into line, never moving from our new positions of corrected behavior on our part. Making any changes in children's lives must be done with tender care.

14. We have to be careful not to misunderstand our children's bad behaviors. Oftentimes when our children act out with wrong behavior, they are trying to tell us that they are bored and that they are missing something. God never intended for any of us to ever live only physical and mental lives, but most people try to do just that. The result is a dull, boring life that leads people to go seeking desperately for something to satisfy the spiritual need within them they are ignoring. This search can go in many directions and involve many different activities while they seek to fill their need for an exciting, meaningful life. Lately I have been very aware of the extent to which the entertainment industry goes in its attempt to entertain people and give them a thrill. What happened to the day when someone just stood on a stage and sang a song and that was enough? Now, you have to sing, dance (often strangely, I might add), dress in bizarre outfits, have fireworks going off and do whatever else you can dream up to get people to watch you. It seems that we have to keep going further and further into the weird to try to keep people interested. What is it people are looking for? They are looking for something to satisfy the need in their soul that cannot be found by any means than a relationship with God. This desperate search for satisfaction is oftentimes why people go so far into destructive behavior that

ruins their lives. There is nothing in this physical world that will ever meet the inner need every man, woman, and child has in their spirit. The life everyone is trying to obtain is spiritual life. People who have real relationships with God will tell you that there is no greater thrill, and that their souls are satisfied with the wonderful life God brings to them. It is pretty amazing to walk and talk with the God of the universe. The empty spirit is the place from which the cry for satisfaction is coming. Until people look to the God who created them for the spiritual life they need, they will stay on their frustrating journey, searching for what they cannot find in anything else. Children hear the cry in their spirit for life louder than adults because they have not yet become accustomed to the practice of stifling it. Some of their bad behavior is due to their boredom with the life we are handing them. Kids are defined by growing, changing, and learning about life, and the oftentimes mundane existence we offer them is not acceptable to them. They know that something is missing and they try to tell us by any means they can. Frequently we misunderstand them and give them a punishment or a prescription to make them stop telling us the truth about their state.

15. There are times when someone tries to teach about grace (offering forgiveness without punishment), those listening turn too far towards leniency and the situation is just as out of balance as it had been when we were living by the letter of the law. Remember, even when you are not what you should be as a parent, your child still needs to learn and understand that wrong acts will bring about bad consequences. That is the reality of this world. We would not be helping our children learn the truth of what they will face in this world if we would not teach them this reality. Yes, there is much we cannot expect out of our children because we have not given them what they needed, but we should begin where we are right now and ask God for the wisdom (James 1:5) to teach our children the proper consequences for their actions. We can find our answers in the Lord; after all, He created love, the family, parents, and children.

He knows what we need to know in order to fix our problems and make our lives function correctly.

16. Parents are either screamers, working from fear and trying to control, or instructors of their children working from wisdom and trying to understand them. Many parents resort to screaming at their children when they are frustrated. I am sorry to admit that I myself have been a screamer at times. We resort to screaming and yelling when we are afraid we cannot control certain situations with our children. Anytime fear is at work in our parenting, we run the risk of losing control of ourselves. Our attempts to control situations only lead to us losing control. As parents, we are not meant to control our children like little robots. We are supposed to instruct them in making wise choices in their lives by helping them to see and feel the consequences of those choices. Children who are constantly controlled will feel robbed of their ability to be their own independent person. What will these children do when they go out on their own if all they have ever known is being controlled? These children will be unable to trust in their own ability to make choices. Providing our children with freedom to make their own choices relays a message to them that they have value as individuals. We need to be instructors as parents. Instructors work from the wisdom they have acquired to try to understand the situations and the children involved and to guide children into making wise choices. We need to understand the difference here. We should not seek to control our children, but to understand our children in the context of the situations that they are facing and instruct them in making proper choices. The need to control will lead to frustration, which sometimes leads to screaming. The frustration comes because people have a built-in need to fight to the death to keep their freedom of choice. Children will fight their parents to keep this freedom. Instruction, however, signals that we respect people's lives and are trying to help them make good choices that will benefit them. In this way we can be seen by the children as helpers rather than ruling dictators. Who of us wants to live under a dictatorship, one where

one's freedom of choice is taken away? We, Americans, fight for the freedom to choose how we live our lives. Why should we as parents who love living in this free country turn around and take away this freedom from our children? When we realize that our goal is not to control our children, but to instruct them, the screaming will stop–along with much of their resistance toward us.

17. My daughter has a horse and reads a lot about how to care for it. I was struck with awe one day as she shared with me what she learned about what will make a horse respond the way you want, a principle found in Mark Rashid's book, *Horses Never Lie*. She said that a horse needs two things from you: to feel secure in your presence and to receive comfort from you. Feeling secure in your presence involves learning to trust you in all situations. Receiving comfort from you means you have the ability to bring peace and happiness to the horse. She explained that when horses do not feel secure with their owners or riders, the fight-or-flight response can kick in, possibly leading to injury. Also, when the horse does not get comfort from its owner, the horse looks to the barn or other horses for that comfort and will fail to bond with or work well with you. Similarly, security and comfort are what people want from God and what children need from their parents. God has much to say about these two qualities in His Word. He clearly counts both as top priority on the list of people's needs and tells us how He provides both security and comfort for us. If God counts these as important and gives them to us, then we parents should be giving these same assets to our children. We need to find ways to communicate security and comfort to our children during every available opportunity. Let me provide a good example of a father providing a sense of security for his children. When I was a little girl my father decided we were going to build a fence around the front of our property. Our family went into the woods and cut down trees to construct the fence. Our finished enclosure was very rustic looking but I remember thinking it was great. When my dad died at the age of 58, I had many thoughts and feelings running through my head

and heart about him. As I tried to deal with this loss, I realized my dad passing away was like having the fence gone in our family. The fence we built together took on new significance. I began to reflect on how I always felt protected by my dad's presence and suddenly that was gone. I can't put my finger on any one thing he did to make me feel this way. I just knew that the way my father lived his life made a safe place for me and if I was in trouble he would come to the rescue. I think he was a great example of a father's protective spirit giving his children a sense of security. When a horse owner provides security and comfort for his or her horse, the animal trusts the person and bonds with him or her, thereby producing a positive, safe, and enjoyable partnership. Similarly, providing security and comfort for our children will foster healthy relationships between parents and children.

Chapter 13

Things Can Be Different

In creation we see the miracle of change every day. The seasons, plants growing in our gardens, and even our faces in the mirror every morning show us the existence and power of change in the world that God created. Living things are always growing and changing. When they stop, they die. However, no one ever said growth and change are always comfortable.

I have written much about what we as parents and our societies are doing wrong with our children and the changes we need to make. This change is not easy to come by. Picture a caterpillar transforming into a butterfly. Change involves discomfort and struggle, things most of us would rather not experience. When we try to change and fail, many of us just give up. I do not think that anyone could work harder to change themselves than I have, and I do not think that anyone could be more frustrated than I was with the results. It was like I was banging my head against the wall. Even when I overcame something, after a while, there it would be again, popping its head up in my life and showing its ugly face. Then I would have to fight it all over again. It was impossible. I would look at the Word of God and see what I was supposed to be like and when I tried to live up to it, I would fall flat on my face. I lived in the try/fail cycle for years, growing more and more discouraged.

Romans 7:13-25 tells us that Jesus is the answer to this struggle. I found Him to be just that in so many ways. Thank God for His kind instruction that is there to help us. I would like to share some keys God has given me that open the door to the power of seeing change happen.

In attempting to become a better parent, we will need to hang on to hope while we endeavor to make changes. Much failure in life comes from situations in which people think they are stuck in the way things are at that moment. They cannot see any hope of things changing and therefore they just sit down where they are, give up, and quite often turn bitter. If we do that, life will decay to misery for us and for those connected to us. Of course, we do not want that for ourselves, our families, or our children. Better parenting comes through hope for the future to be different.

We have to actively attack our problems with hope–the hope that we will find the answer and that things will change, just as God promises:

> Call unto me, and I will answer thee, and show thee
> great and mighty things, which thou knowest not.
> Jer. 3:33

Even when everything is the same (or worse) day after day, day in and day out, we need to accept that things will change in our mind, plant our feet in hope, and refuse to give in to despair.

If we are going to overcome a problem in our lives, we have to be more persistent in believing that it will go than the problem is at staying in our lives. The more persistent thought will always win out when it comes to the reality of living. Failure happens when we let the persistence of our problem move us from our place of hope. Using the promises of God's Word, we need to convince ourselves that our new way of thinking will win out over the wrong way of thinking. We can change our thoughts from hopelessness to belief that change will happen. Even while we persist in the wrong behavior, we have to settle it in our minds and refuse to believe anything else but the fact that we will change. We can make faith work by cooperating with it. We must not fight against faith by despairing.

One important article of faith to remember when taking this stand is "Let God be God." So many of us try to play God in life when we try to change ourselves and others via our own power. When trying to change others, know that there is not a human being alive who can get into the heart of another person and change it. Trying to do this will frustrate us to no end. The person will resist our control over them to the point of death. We need to save that thought and use it when dealing with our children. We have to work on other things, but God does the work on the heart.

> … for thou only knowest the hearts of the children of men. 2 Chron. 6:30

Changing people is God's business. He alone can go to the hearts of human beings and effect change. He has done it over and over again throughout time. We need to trust God to change us and others and get out of His way so He can do it. It takes believing that He wants to do this work

> A new heart also will I give you, and a new spirit will I put within you: and I will take away the stony heart out of your flesh, and I will give you an heart of flesh. Ezek. 36:26

and He can do this work.

> … according as His divine power hath given unto us all things that pertain unto life and godliness, through the knowledge of Him that hath called us to glory and virtue. 1 Pet. 1:3

Have you ever tried to help your child do something you knew he could not do alone, only to be told by your child that you are not to help him? He wants to do it himself, and he tries, and he fails. There you stand ready and able to assist, but your help is refused. You feel very sad that your child has to experience failure because he will not let you instruct him. That is exactly how God must feel when we keep trying to change ourselves and others. God has far more ability to see what is wrong and how to fix it than we do. He has promised us the resurrection power of Jesus Christ to do the work of changing us from ways of death to ways of life.

> But if the spirit of him that raised up Jesus from the dead dwell in you, He that raised up Christ from the dead shall also quicken your mortal bodies by His Spirit that dwelleth in you. Rom. 8:11

Do we have this kind of power (the power that raises people from the dead to life again) in our hands? No! God does, though, and that is exactly the power He uses to work changes in us. It works! We have to stop trying to change the situation and let God do it. That involves our cooperation, not our control. Our cooperation does not mean we just sit like blobs and do nothing. We cooperate and agree with God as He does the work.

It helped me, in my struggle, to understand this truth: God (the Father, Jesus the Son, and the Holy Spirit) does the work of change in us so He can get the glory, not us. Why do we think we will be praising Him for all eternity? Every time He worked a change in my heart, I was completely amazed. My efforts were worthless at modifying my behavior with any lasting results. I would just slip right back into the same old ruts of thinking and acting that my past had made. But God knew exactly what thoughts and circumstances had to come into my life in order for the change to come about. I watched Him do it so many times and have truly come to understand that His ways are not my ways and His thoughts are not my thoughts (Isa. 55:8). I tell Him all the time, "I will be praising You in eternity forever and ever because of what I have seen You do to this old rebellious heart of mine." Even now, every time I remember how He has worked a change in my life, I start praising Him. What complete joy to see our stubborn bad behavior, which brought misery and trouble into our lives, be replaced by good, godly behavior. God brought us to know salvation through His son, Jesus Christ, and He is faithful to finish the work by perfecting us by His power.

> Being confident of this very thing, that, he which hath begun a good work in you will perform (complete) it until the day of Jesus Christ. Phil. 1:6

Things can be different. You can change, but only through the power of God. I tell you this to save you from the sorrow of trying and trying again and failing. Many people throw in the towel of faith at this point of frustration. It is not about you trying, but about you trusting God and cooperating with what He is doing in your life. Giving up is not an option. Just like love, mentioned in Chapter 10, it is not about how many times you fall flat on your face in attempts to change. It is about getting up every time you fall and continuing in faith. Get up, look at Jesus, believe in His resurrection power, and continue to hope that things will change. The day you don't get up is the day you truly fail yourself, your child, your family, and God. God wants good for you. He wants you to have peace, peace being a place of rest from all your troubles. Let Him do the work to get you there.

> For I know the thoughts I think toward you, saith the Lord, thoughts of peace, and not of evil, to give you an expected end. Jer. 29:11

Chapter 14

My Journey to Here

Do you know how many times I laid *The Cry of the Children* aside because I felt I failed so badly with my own children? Fourteen years passed between the time that God told me to write my book to when I finally finished it. I made so many mistakes with my children that I did not feel qualified to advise others. I learned that though I failed, I was learning valuable lessons and becoming a better person and parent through it. I mourn over my children's wounds. This mourning is my true inspiration for writing. I ask my children and God to forgive me. I pray for God to heal my children and help me use what I have learned to spare others the sorrow my children and I have experienced. Maybe if someone else had shared their experiences and the answers they had found my kids would not have suffered the way they did. Thank God He forgives and heals us of our wounds. How else would we survive? I write now not as a perfect parent, but as a perfected parent.

I am writing not from intellect collected in the mind or from facts recorded in other books (except the Bible). I am writing from a burden felt in my spirit–a spirit that has felt the pain of being denied the essentials for survival in this world. This book is birthed from the tears brought by the sorrow felt when a child is wounded, hurt, neglected, and uncared for in his or her spirit and then made to live its life with that pain and deficiency. You are reading it now because the cry of unkempt souls is so loud that it can no longer be ignored. The neglect of the children today is the failure of the world tomorrow.

Will you be someone who hears the cry of the children and becomes part of the solution or someone who continues to be part of the reason for the cry? I believe that your answer to that question holds the key to your destiny. If you are not part of the solution, you very well may reap the consequences of the problem. Crying children become very angry and destructive adults.

If we say, "Yes, I do care," then will we change the way we view the situation and see the real source of the problem, even if it is in us? Will we stop attacking our youth's behavior and start looking for the root cause of it? Do we all have enough courage to do that? It is not a blame/shame game. It instead is a "Let's-work-together-to-heal-the-helpless" plan.

I loved my children enough to start this journey, even when it meant taking me apart and remaking my whole personality and way of living. I've had to rip out ways of thinking and acting and it caused me great pain, but they had been wreaking havoc on my children's spirits, so I had to change them. I am just an ordinary person who has asked God for help. If I can do it, so can you. It will be healing to your spirit. You see, usually whatever is in your spirit bringing destruction to your children, is a negative force at work in you anyway. You've just kept it so long inside of you that you do not recognize it for what it is. Your healing is your child's health.

One point I think we all need to understand when viewing someone who has written a book about knowledge they have acquired: just because they have keen insight into a certain subject doesn't mean they have arrived on the train at the land of perfect people. They have just climbed one mountain in life and now can see the many more mountain peaks they must scale. It is all about helping others up the mountain with them so that they can go on with their journey. Another mountain peak awaits me, but I know who brought me up this one and He'll faithfully see me to the end because He tells me:

> Teaching them to observe all things that I have commanded you; and lo, I am with you always, even to the end of the age. Matt. 28:30

Chapter 15

The Best Thing You Can Do For Your Child

In my observations of my own parenting and others, I have noticed that those of us lacking love and acceptance from our childhood tend to spend our adult lives continuing to look for something to meet that need. We sometimes seem very centered on ourselves and our wants. We can be so self-absorbed in our own state of lack that we do not even notice or care about the needs of others. Many times in raising my children, I just did not have anything to give to their spirits. Out of what would I give it? I was empty. My need to be loved and accepted gnawed at me, making me spend most of my time and energy trying to relieve my own pain. Only when I found what I needed in God was I able to see to the needs of my children. When our needs are met, we are then able to give to others. We can take the attention away from us and look to the needs those who need our care. Parenting is a time to concentrate on the needs of the little ones dependent on us for their well-being. We must have something to give them or we will just produce more needy, self-centered souls. I am giving you the answer I found to my need. God gave me the love and acceptance I lacked. My empty soul was finally filled and I could now give to those who needed something from me–my dear children. As we read in Matthew 10:27, when God tells us something, we are to preach it from the housetops. *The Cry of the Children* is my way of doing this. I want us to have the needs of our soul and spirit met so that we can be whole and can then tend to the needs of the precious children with whom we are blessed.

I am very sad to say that, in my life and ministry, I have met many people who have lived out their lives and never found answers to their needs. Below is a sincere message from my parent's heart to yours. We are God's dear children, and He can provide everything we need. We, in turn, can provide our children with what they need.

We must first understand that we each have a spirit that requires care. We are living from that spirit every moment of every day. We are living out our lives among other people, and the way we live has an impact on us and those with whom we live. The best thing we, parents, can do for our children is to take care of our own spirits first. We cannot do anything about what care was received in the past, but we can start now and seek healing and restoration.

Why should we think that the spiritual part of our life is so important? Jesus spoke very loudly from the cross when He gave up His life. The care of your spirit was so important to Him that He gave up his physical life, His earthly existence, to give us all spiritual life. By His death, He showed us what was more important–life for our spirit. It is worth losing everything else for spiritual life.

> For what profit is it to a man if he gains the whole world, and loses his own soul? Or what will a man give in exchange for his soul? Matt. 16:26

The following verses give you a guideline for how to begin your spiritual life with God. Many people I know have followed this path and found real life, which is clearly seen by their changed and happy lives.

- God says in His Word the way to spiritual life is found in Him.

God created you with an eternal spirit that has been made to dwell with Him (eternal life). You will never be whole until you make that connection.

> And they [Adam and Eve] heard the voice of the Lord God walking in the garden in the cool of the day… And the Lord God called unto Adam and said, "Where art thou?" Gen. 3:8-9

> So the Lord spoke to Moses face to face, as a man speaks to his friend. Exod. 33:11

> Behold, I stand at the door, and knock: If any man hears my voice, and opens the door, I will come in to him, and will sup with him, and he with me. Rev. 3:20

> That which we have seen and heard declare we unto you, that ye also may have fellowship with us: and truly our fellowship is with the Father, and with His Son Jesus Christ. 1 John 1:3

- The connection between God and man is possible through faith in God's Son, Jesus Christ.

> He that hath the Son hath life; and he that hath not the Son of God hath not life. 1 John 1:12

> That whosoever believeth in Him (Jesus Christ) should not perish, but have eternal life. John 3:15

- That connection is not possible without Jesus because we have sinful, wayward hearts that separate us from our Holy God.

> But your iniquities have separated between you and your God, and your sins have hid His face from you, that He will not hear. Isa. 59:2

All we like sheep have gone astray; we have turned everyone to his own way; and the Lord hath laid on Him the iniquity of us all. Isa. 53:6

- On our best day, doing the best we've ever done, we would not be good enough to make ourselves right with God.

    For all have sinned and come short of the glory of God. Rom. 3:23

- His standard is higher than ours.

    For as the heavens are higher than the earth, so are my ways higher than your ways, and my thoughts than your thoughts. Isa. 55:9

- Adam and Eve set the stage for all mankind to follow sin, therefore resulting in this separation from God.

    Wherefore, as by one man (Adam) sin entered into the world, and death by sin; and so death passed upon all men, for that all have sinned. Rom. 5:12

- Our spirits are therefore empty of life (spiritually dead). God only holds our spiritual life.

    But of the tree of the knowledge of good and evil, thou shalt not eat of it: for in the day that thou eatest thereof thou shalt surely die. Gen. 2:17

- God had already set the stage for all mankind to be saved from this death by having His Son, Jesus, die and give His life to take our punishment and pay for our sins.

    Unto Him [Jesus Christ] that loved us, and washed us from our sins in His own blood. Rev. 1:5b

- God our Creator, our Father, loved us enough to make a way for us to get to Him when we could not do it in our own ability.

  But God commandeth His love toward us, in that, while we were yet sinners, Christ died for us. Rom. 5:8

- It cost God His most precious possession, His Son. There is no greater love.

  For God so loved the world, that He gave His only begotton Son, that whosoever believeth in Him should not perish, but have everlasting life. John 3:16

- Jesus gave His life willingly for us to have our relationship with God restored. He knows that we have no life outside of that. He loved us too.

  … that we, being dead to sins, should live unto righteousness: by whose stripes ye were healed. 1 Pet. 2:24

  For the Son of man is come to seek and to save that which was lost. Luke 19:10

  Behold the Lamb of God, which taketh away the sin of the world. John 1:29

- Our responsibility, when we hear this truth, is to believe that God loves us and to receive His answer to the problem in our spirits.

  How shall they believe in Him of whom they have not heard? Rom. 10:14

  Most assuredly, I say to you, he who believes in Me [Jesus Christ] has everlasting life. John 6:47

But as many as received Him, to them He gave the right to become children of God, to those who believe in His name. John 1:12

- We are to call on Jesus Christ to save us from our sins that keep us from God, our spiritual Father.

  For whoever calls on the name of the Lord shall be saved. Rom. 10:13

- We must admit that we are incapable of ever saving ourselves from our sinful state by any good deeds that we do and that Jesus Christ has saved us through His death on the cross.

  If we confess our sin, He is faithful and just to forgive us our sins and to cleanse us from all unrighteousness. 1 John 1:9

  That if you confess with your mouth the Lord Jesus Christ and believe in your heart that God has raised Him from the dead, you will be saved. Rom. 10:9

- When we do this, we have our relationship with God restored and life comes to our spirit.

  Much more then, being now justified by His blood, we shall be saved from wrath through Him. For if, when we were enemies, we were reconciled to God by the death of His Son, much more, being reconciled, we shall be saved by His life. And not only so, but we also joy in God through our Lord Jesus Christ, by whom we have now received the atonement [reconciliation]. Rom. 5:9-11

  And God hath both raised up the Lord, and will also raise up us by His power. 1 Cor. 6:14

And ye shall know that I am the Lord, when I have opened you graves, O my people, and brought you up out of your graves, And shall put my spirit in you, and you shall live, and I shall place ye in your own land: then shall ye know that I the Lord have spoken it, and preformed it, saith the Lord. Ezek. 37:13-14

- We are now members of God's beloved family and that is a forever membership.

  Beloved, now are we the sons of God… John 3:2

  The Spirit itself beareth witness with our spirit, that we are the children of God. Rom. 7:16

  These things have I written unto you that believe on the name of the Son of God; that ye many know that ye have eternal life… 1 John 5:13

  And this is the promise that He hath promised us, even eternal life. 1 John 2:25

- Our spirits now, being made right and clean through the blood of Jesus Christ, are the place God sends His Holy Spirit to reside. Jesus is speaking:

  And I will pray the Father and He shall give you another Comforter (helper), that He may abide with you forever. John 14:16

  Nevertheless I tell you the truth, it is to your advantage that I go away, for if I do not go away, the Helper will not come to you; but if I depart, I will send Him to you. John 16:7

  Then Peter said to them, Repent, and be baptized every

one of you in the Name of Jesus Christ for the remissions [forgiveness] of sins, and ye shall receive the gift of the Holy Ghost. Acts 2:38

- We now have a personal trainer to lead us into all truth (God's way).

  Howbeit when He, the Spirit of truth, is come, He will guide you into all truth… John16:13

  But the Comforter, which is the Holy Ghost, whom the Father will send in my name, He shall teach you all things, and bring all things to your remembrance, whatsoever I have said to you. Luke 14:26

  For He Himself has said, I will never leave you nor forsake you. So we may boldly say: The Lord is my helper. Heb. 13:5-6

God draws you to Himself by His great love for you.
Jesus saves you by His great act of sacrifice for you.
The Holy Spirit keeps you by His great presence in you.

Epilogue
Crying Children

by Kitty Havener

God, the children are crying.
I can see the sadness in their eyes.
I hear the cry coming from their spirit.
They are weeping in their souls.
It is a long and heartfelt cry.
It goes on and on through time.
Their cries come up from the earth to your throne.
Your heart is moved for their need.
Why do they cry?
They weep because they hurt inside.
They feel empty and lost.
They don't know who they are
or where they are going.
They don't know their value or purpose.
They have a hunger inside that no one seems to be able to fill.
They cry on and on.
No one seems to be able to make them stop.

We try to distract them with everything we can get our hands on.
We try to talk them out of crying.
They annoy us with their crying.
Some of us remember when we cried like them.
Then, we got busy living our lives and forgot to listen to the pain in our souls.
The children can still hear the cry, loud and clear.
Their honesty is still alive.
Who is going to do something about the crying children?
Will someone stop, listen, and care enough to help?
Maybe, just maybe, it is what God cares about the most.
There is a crying child close to you.
Stop and listen
Maybe it is you.

Printed in the United States
By Bookmasters